IMPACTFUL FACILITY MANAGEMENT

ALI ALSUWAIDI

PASSIONPRENEUR®
PUBLISHING

IMPACTFUL FACILITY MANAGEMENT

How to Conceptualise and
Implement Contemporary Best
Practices and Automation-Driven
Facilities Transformation

ALI ALSUWAIDI

PASSIONPRENEUR®
P U B L I S H I N G

Publishing information
Publishing and design facilitated by Passionpreneur Publishing
A division of Passionpreneur Organization Pty Ltd
ABN: 48640637529

Melbourne, VIC | Australia
www.PassionpreneurPublishing.com

To my beloved mother, who gave me joy and direction, and to my late father, whose pride made me reach for great things. May Allah rest his soul.

To my wife, the greatest blessing Allah gave me, who is always there for me, and to our four amazing children, Maitha, Majed, Khalid and Zayed. To Mohamed Al Mulla, my best friend of 30+ years.

And finally, to the unforgettable people who I have worked with over my career. This book is for you, and for all facility managers and industry peers in the Middle East and worldwide who believe in the industry and have supported me all the way.

Together we can!

TABLE OF CONTENTS

CHAPTER 1

INTRODUCTION

Facility Management integrates multiple disciplines, forming a singular strategy and processes that help achieve the efficiency and productivity of economies of countries, cities and organisations while having a positive impact on the health, well-being and quality of life of individuals (ISO 41001:2018). "FM" is the widely accepted acronym for facility management which I will use at various places in this book.

The primary thought which has prompted this book is my belief that while the impact of FM is huge, its principles and best practices have not been applied to their full extent! My intent with this book is to quantify the impact of FM in detail and convey the importance of ensuring that FM best practices are applied appropriately, especially in megaprojects where prudent FM approaches can be a key success factor.

"IT IS VERY IMPORTANT TO HAVE A FEEDBACK LOOP, WHERE YOU'RE CONSTANTLY THINKING ABOUT WHAT YOU HAVE DONE AND HOW YOU COULD BE DOING IT BETTER".

- ELON MUSK

Megaprojects are defining a new course in built environments. These types of projects, characterised by large-scale integrated township-style developments, are assuming greater share of the real estate landscape across the world. Well-delivered facility management becomes key to ensuring business excellence and sustainability, which is encapsulated by Elon Musk's statement. It is only when a culture of collaborative thinking and continuous improvement is applied, that the world can achieve its aim of efficient, sustainable developments that leave a mark for generations to come.

I am regularly asked for my opinion on which facility management company is the best in the region, or how to establish service specifications to optimise the value of operating facilities. The answer is not simple! It requires leadership and passion to drive FM strategy to achieve such objectives. Feedback loops, continuous improvement and conceptualising a service solution with an exact fit to user requirements, are critical success factors for becoming a leader in the FM industry.

A key secret lies in understanding the needs and optimising the use of technology. Through this book, I aim to take you through the journey of understanding how implementing FM best practices, equipped with technology, can maximise impact on the total cost of ownership and related lifecycle stages. In this context, my focus is particularly on megaprojects and beyond. FM optimisation and impact is not easily achievable in a megaproject since it involves diverse stakeholders, with different objectives, through the various lifecycle stages of a development.

This book aims to help readers understand how to capture learnings and create feedback loops to improve sustainability aspects, and quality of life for users of existing and future developments. These teachings are informed by my 25-plus years of experience in diverse aspects of facility management.

I would like to focus my message in this book on the top three learnings of my career:

- Establishing FM strategies driven by continuous improvement to maximise financial and nonfinancial benefits
- Enabling visibility of the various pain points of users and stakeholders such as the owner and service providers through the various lifecycle stages of a development
- Creating data and technology-driven strategies to maximise the benefits of FM best practices on the total cost of ownership

As a passionate and senior FM industry professional engaged with all stakeholders over the various lifecycle stages of developments across the region, I would like to share with you my vision of revolution in the FM industry. This vision is similar to the revolution in the automobile industry, where introducing sustainable electrical vehicles is creating the next big disruption and transforming a key aspect of our lives: mobility. As the many examples from this comparable industry indicate, successful strategies can only be implemented when backed by the right leadership, a sense of passion and the drive to transform.

For close to three decades now, I have been in pursuit of defining the right strategy for success in transformation through facility management. In addition to my observations on general trends in FM, my intent with this book is to offer owners and operators of megaprojects insights into starting and establishing your successful journey in modern-day facility operations and asset management.

I also hope I can inspire young FM practitioners as they embark on the journey to becoming the next generation of FM leaders!

CHAPTER 2

THE STORY OF FM IMPACT

Through the Lens of a 25-Year Journey

It was in the summer of 1997 when, freshly armed with an electrical engineering degree from the University of Toledo, I stood at the cusp of my first major career decision. This was also the time that the world was at its own inflection point: discovering a whole new realm of global connectivity ushered in by the internet. With several opportunities in traditional and contemporary engineering practices, I chose to pursue a career in power plant operations and maintenance with a premier telecom service provider. After five years in this role, I assumed a position in the Health, Safety & Security department, driven by the desire to make a real difference to the wellness and protection of people, especially those who work in the field.

After a few months into this health & safety role, I wondered whether I was truly making a difference. Even small instances of non-conformance to established health & safety norms made me wonder why there was resistance to change, and why I couldn't make the impact I envisaged. It seemed that every time I highlighted non-conformances after a health and safety review of a facility or called for an audit, it was met with groans and grumbles – like I was asking people to waste an enormous amount of time on something trivial. What irked me most in my early career was why my work and contribution to the company wasn't appreciated as much as it should have been.

I had conversations with my supervisors about this dilemma. What one senior, seasoned colleague told me has stayed with me ever since – but more about that a little later.

Twenty-three years later in the summer of 2020, with a global pandemic raging and causing unbelievable disruptions in every aspect of our lives, FM professionals, driven by sound principles of health and safety, were hailed as heroes. As the group of professionals who got the wheels of our economies rolling again by enabling the safe reopening of societies: workplaces, residential communities, social, healthcare and every other aspect we had taken for granted prior to the pandemic. With this health and safety grounding, FM professionals have emerged as champions of responsible behaviour in the built environment. From being a standard question way down in most tender documents (and usually included as a formality), queries about health and safety expertise are now top priority capability asked of bidders. Once called an innocuous "HSE", today the practice is referred to as Health, Safety, Environment and Sustainability – indicating its role as a harbinger of the way real estate is making real, long-term impact for generations to come.

THIS REMINDED ME OF WHAT THAT WISE SENIOR HAD ADVISED ME, "IT'S NOT UNTIL IT GOES AWAY THAT PEOPLE REALISE THE VALUE OF SOMETHING THAT THEY TAKE FOR GRANTED".

It sounds like a cliché but consider this – how much thought do we give, while getting on an aeroplane, to the many hours of work that goes into designing, manufacturing, maintaining and flying a machine that holds the lives of so many? How often have we appreciated the work of aerospace professionals who are responsible for ensuring that we land safely at our destinations?

And now imagine, for one moment, life without air travel. Everything from the leisure and hospitality industries, to global trade, would come to a grinding halt. It's the same about FM as a practice – it goes beyond just well-oiled engineering equipment and clean washrooms. It defines the very soul of the building.

THE IMPACT OF FM

This context alone defines the importance of understanding the impact of facility management. Therefore, this book is all about the **impact** of facility management. Because, when you think about it, asset management and facility operations have a truly far-reaching impact.

Impact point
Smart Societies

Automation and digital integration are changing the way we engage with diverse aspects of daily life requirements. Deep technology integration with built environments is driving the move towards smart societies which make everyday lives more efficient

Impact point
Wellness

Real estate strategies, material innovation and practices are all driving the touchpoints of human health, wellness and lifestyle. Facility operations impact how we enable wellness in our everyday lives through extraneous influences

Impact point
Commercial

Whether the creation of a community that draws the ideal user base, enhanced tenancy periods through user satisfaction, or optimised cost of operations without compromise on user experience, FM practices have a strong top-line and bottom-line impact on real estate operations

Impact point
Ecology

Sustainability is a key outcome of modern-day FM operations. Alignment to global sustainability standards helps real estate developments contribute to global efforts on climate control and other ecological aspects

While these impact points are true of all built environments and real estate developments of all scales, they assume specific importance and amplification in the case of megaprojects, where the quantum of FM impact – whether positive or negative – is much higher and the opportunities to contribute to socio-economic growth a lot more.

This book is an encapsulation of how to think through, and implement strategies that lead to Impactful FM across megaprojects and beyond.

CHAPTER 3

DEFINING THE SOUL

Leadership Lessons in FM Start
with Learning the Right Way to Grow
the Industry Responsibly

In the 1950s, a group of Japanese architects started a thought movement called Metabolism – a philosophy that promoted the concept of buildings as living beings. In their manifesto for this movement, the group used biological comparisons to propose that buildings are capable of regeneration and fit into the framework of a "new urbanism". The theory isn't very far-fetched and, although Metabolism isn't a widely discussed concept anymore, its core principles remain relevant. This is especially true in the context of modern building technologies and the emergence of megaprojects.

At the surface level, buildings are inanimate objects – a collection of building materials held together by bonding agents. If we delve deeper, buildings are not that different from living beings. The ideal building interacts and engages with its occupiers and adapts to their changing needs and requirements. Today, there is an emerging trend in architectural design termed "adaptive buildings". Adaptive built environments are those capable of embracing conditions as they emerge – much like living organisms.

Therefore, like any other living organism, buildings need a "soul" – an essence that defines them. This soul of the built environment is facility management. Tasked conceptually with keeping the essence of the building intact, FM integrates multiple disciplines to influence the efficiency and user-friendliness of buildings.

I have learnt this essential role of FM throughout my 25-year career. Experts aren't born, they are made – I started as a trainee in the operation and maintenance department. Today, I'm the Vice Chairperson of the Global FM association and an expert in megaprojects and high-rise buildings. The learning curve between then and now has been steep, but I have always been passionate about the FM industry, and this has propelled my career.

Passion is the primary trait that enables an FM professional to emerge as a leader in the sector. Indeed, with passion and vision, leaders will drive the future of the industry as we continue to come together, especially in high-growth geographies, like the Middle East region.

WHAT MAKES AN FM PROFESSIONAL AN IMPACT AGENT

To become an FM expert, you must first be empathetic. That is, having the ability to understand the pain and frustrations of others, especially that of customers / end-users and the industry itself in a regional context. This has been a core focus of mine from the start because I want the Middle Eastern region to lead the world in FM excellence and sustainability practices. This means constantly looking differently at what we do and being able to think innovatively.

It is important to make sure that all subject matter experts within this region work together to advance the FM industry and its impact on existing and future developments. My role has and will continue to bring people together!

They say that one hour of planning can save us ten hours of doing. I have come to accept this as a core truth of all that we do. Failing to plan is planning to fail! This is a fundamental tenet of sustainable development, where the role of FM consultancy should be embedded in the planning phase so it can help us to achieve sustainable development in projects – especially megaprojects – from day one!

WHY I SELECTED MEGAPROJECTS FOR THIS BOOK

Given their scale and complexity, megaprojects are the pinnacle of FM excellence. A megaproject is typically defined as a project that exceeds USD 1 billion in development cost. However, they are more complex to define than with a numerical threshold. Flyvbjerg (2009) defined megaprojects as construction projects that consider a specific investment context with their cost threshold ranging between USD 500 million and 1 billion. Aside from large-scale investments, megaprojects are usually characterised by (1) political sensitivity (Locatelli and Mancini 2010); (2) long delivery span (usually over four years), which includes planning, design, and construction (Merrow 1988; Oliomogbe and Smith 2012); (3) high complexity (Haynes 2002; Fiori and Kovaka 2005); (4) high risks (Flyvbjerg et al. 2003; Fiori and Kovaka 2005); and (5) a large number of internal and external project stakeholders (Oliomogbe and Smith 2012). In some geographies, one notable example being China, most construction megaprojects are broken down into several constituent projects, which are then executed separately.

From an FM and sustainability aspect, we look not only at development cost (which is only 20% of the total cost of ownership) but also capture the whole lifecycle cost and total cost of ownership.

Total cost of ownership (TCO) is generally defined as the creation or purchase price of an asset plus the costs of operating and maintaining the asset till it is disposed of. In the context of real estate and built environments, TCO is the cost of development, including design and construction, plus costs associated with asset maintenance, facility operations and refurbishments as the major cost heads.

Assessing TCO represents the bigger picture of examining from the perspective of a product's value over time. The figure below defines the concept of the total cost of ownership in built environments.

Facility Cost Category	Project Lifetime	Lifetime Cost
	Years 30-40 ➤	
Planning, Design and Construction		10-20%
Maintenance & Operations		50-70%
Capital Renewal		20-30%
Demolition		1%

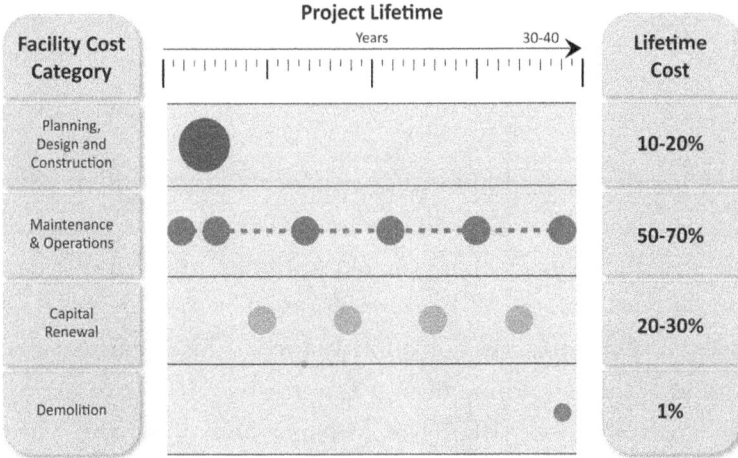

My simple definition of a megaproject considering all of the aspects defined above, is one that costs upwards of half a billion dollars to develop, and has a total cost of ownership of USD 2.5 billion (USD 500,000,000 as development cost × 5).

Urban centres, much like buildings, can be viewed in the context of Metabolism. If anything, they behave most like living organisms. I like to compare buildings to amoebae – adapting themselves to shapes that suit rapidly evolving socioeconomic and human demands. Today, most cities are emerging as a collection of megaprojects. This is especially true of the Middle East which offers significant opportunity for urban redevelopment, driven by the levels of economic activity, highly adaptable residents and visionary leaders. Examples of such megaprojects within broader city visions include Dubai Marina, which has been master-planned as a megaproject, and King Abdullah Financial District which is an exciting megaproject within the city of Riyadh in the Kingdom of Saudi Arabia.

The meteoric rise of Dubai city as a world-leading metropolis and the leader of innovative urban development is the result of an amazing journey of commitment and innovation, which has started to bear exceptional results in the last twenty years. One major contributor to this emergence of Dubai is the development of megaprojects such as Jumeirah Beach Residence (JBR), The Marina, Dubai Internet City, Dubai Media City, Jumeirah Lakes Towers, Burj Khalifa Downtown and others. Developed as independent mini townships over the past 10 years, these megaprojects are coming together to transform Dubai into a global centre of iconic sustainable developments. This is only possible through the impact of a sustainable FM strategy within these megaprojects. Dubai's approach is a beacon for cities worldwide to adopt and emulate.

In the course of my career in FM, I have been fortunate to witness the development of path-breaking iconic megaproject developments including:

Jumeirah Beach Residence	The single biggest development of its scale. Built in only four years with 36 towers (of G+50 and more) over 6 podiums
Jebel Ali Free Zone	100 km+ of roads with mixed-use warehouses, offices and staff accommodation seamlessly integrated with the Jebel Ali port
Ibn Battuta Mall, Gardens and Discovery Gardens	1.5 million square feet of retail, apartments, villas, offices and hotels with a community capacity of 100,000+ people
Dubai International Financial Centre	High-end offices for 400+ financial firms integrated with retail, F&B and hotels
Downtown Burj Khalifa	Mega development with an estimated construction cost of USD 20 billion for the entire development
CMA Tower, King Abdullah Financial District	An iconic 80-storey crystalline office tower
Palm Jumeirah	Developed at an estimated construction cost of USD 30 billion for the entire development

Being part of the FM process for these developments, in some capacity, has helped me understand the intricacies of what makes megaprojects great: true socioeconomic, commercial and sustainability impact.

Cities emerging as a collection of megaprojects is an impressive trend. Imagine if we fix chronic issues in mini city developments by applying FM strategy and related best practices at all stages of their lifecycle – we will get extraordinary results as a complete urban centre!

A VISION TRANSLATING INTO REAL OUTCOMES

When I joined the FM industry and learnt more about FM best practices, and the related impact on the economy, this became my vision and drive. My passion became clearer when I saw the huge developments taking place in the region between 2000 and 2010. I kept (and keep) asking myself, *how can FM truly impact these megaprojects?* How can we influence the total cost of ownership (and not just the handover and operations stages)?

To achieve this intent, I dove straight into operation and maintenance with a large telecom organisation. To understand my learnings on Impactful FM, it is important to understand my career path. I'd like to provide a disclaimer here that I repeat some of what I had mentioned in earlier pages, but it's important to reiterate this here to set the context. I worked with an established company for eight years, before moving as an FM manager to a newly launched telecom company in the UAE back in 2006. When I subsequently switched positions and began work as the operations director with a leading total FM provider, I had the amazing mandate of applying FM best practices and capitalising on the many learnings from my experience in telecom. At the same time, I aimed to develop a differentiated strategy rather than reapply what I had been doing in past assignments. As part of this effort, I evolved a model where the engagement was structured as a contract, with the company playing the role of an owner's representative, conceptualising and implementing strategies to protect owner interest. This is where I harnessed my combined FM expertise, sense of leadership and passion to apply principles of total FM and gain many benefits through integration. This included better management of risks, improvement in quality, and addressing challenges through frequent management interaction. Beyond this, I have played several roles as the owner FM representative, starting with one of the first government-owned FM companies in the UAE.

My career has therefore afforded me the opportunity to learn from a wide variety of projects, including megaprojects developed for distinct use. I truly cherish the broad range of expertise that has emerged from managing developments as diverse as the Jebel Ali Port and Freezone, Palm Jumeirah, Discovery Gardens (a 380-building community), Ibn Battuta Mall and residential communities around it, and several others. The integrated development masterplans of Discovery Gardens and Ibn Battuta Mall helped me get a feel for large, integrated, planned mixed-use developments, and megaprojects from the very nascent stages of the concept.

But I have also been fortunate to be in the midst of what is probably the most exciting development market in the world – Dubai – at the peak of the market boom. This has helped grow my passion, deepen my understanding of complex facility operations and reinforce the conviction that FM is a key driver of efficiency and sustainability in megaprojects.

But the other message was that, as obvious as the outcomes and benefits may be, the road isn't easy. The biggest roadblock is resistance to change, and the need to take a very diverse set of stakeholders through the journey of doing something new and transformative, while keeping in mind long-term impact and near-term gains. At every stage of my career, I have been challenged by clients to manage costs while improving quality of service. Moreover, I've been challenged by the mandate to manage buildings that have information missing from various systems, leading to a lack of transparency on aspects related to construction, while moving to the operations stage. These challenges occurred while concurrently trying to bridge communication gaps with most clients who are asset owners.

As I navigated these challenges, I sought answers to advancing my vision of creating sustainable developments through impactful FM strategies. As this vision evolved, a few truths became obvious: FM strategy is about facilitating improvement in quality of life, while enhancing core business performance, and creating opportunities for asset owners to grow and protect their brand. Of course, increasingly at the heart of it all is the core pillar of sustainability as part of the development strategy.

This vision of mine was very challenging to achieve in the market mindset pre-2010. At this stage in its evolution, the market was still underdeveloped from an asset and FM perspective. We had challenges and were working with various clients to translate this vision into real outcomes. Most of the time, we either arrived late in the project lifecycle, or could not identify the stakeholders to collaborate with, when putting the strategy together. Ultimately, we faced resistance because people wanted to see results immediately rather than planning and working together over the three to five years it takes to plan and achieve true impact. Despite these conflicts, we stayed committed to the transformation of these megaprojects, working to continually improve strategy and convert them into one-hundred-percent sustainable developments.

I have always endeavoured to use technology in my mission to achieve the impact of FM in these big projects. Ultimately, people and vendors were selling hardware rather than selling solutions and taking advantage of technology as terminology. My first attempt was to connect buildings into one centralised location, gather useful data, qualify people and guide them.

My mission was also to get feedback loops, implemented to understand design stage elements where we could gather information and improve the design criteria, thereby improving the quality of construction from a durability and maintainability point of view. This would ensure that the handover, which I consider more specialised than a normal handover, centres around a building birth certificate – an important step towards creating a sustainable development.

To say it was difficult is putting it mildly. But from this need emerged another important initiative – I realised the need for a collaborative platform to reflect and unify the industry voice. A coming together of voices of all industry stakeholders, where we talk about our pains in an open forum. This is when the leaders of the industry came together to establish the Middle East Facility Management Association (MEFMA) in 2009.

Coincidentally, this was also the time that I transitioned from being a service provider back to an asset owner representative and working on one of the most mega of megaprojects, albeit in the form of a tall building. As the first director of operations for the Burj Khalifa, the world's tallest tower, I had the opportunity to apply a wide range of FM best practices to a megaproject, which in turn was part of a larger development: Downtown Burj Khalifa. In this assignment as Senior Director of Operations, I was chiefly accountable and responsible for managing the transition to completion, and preparing the project for handover.

Being part of the responsibility for an enormous master plan – Downtown Burj Khalifa – was a proud moment for me. Conceptualised as a project spanning an entire kilometre of the most prestigious real estate on earth, the vision was ambitious. Today, you can see how that vision came to fruition. Rarely has human achievement in technology, real estate and lifestyle come together so cohesively as it has in the case of Burj Khalifa.

At the same time, assuming a board member position in MEFMA gave me another distinct mandate: bringing together leaders from different countries in the region to evolve and apply FM best practices, consequently affecting significant government and privately owned asset portfolios – those that we can call mega and giga projects.

Ultimately, this was my attempt to execute the vision of an FM strategy that was so impactful it extended to urban centres and nations, starting with megaprojects. In this context, my experience at Burj Khalifa was most awe-inspiring!

The journey of MEFMA's emergence as a knowledge and collaboration powerhouse is encapsulated in the few photographs here:

INDUSTRY ENGAGEMENT

COMPLETE IMPACT SOLUTIONING FOR MEGAPROJECTS

As part of this journey of industry evolution, I have also continually sought to establish what I believe would be one of my most important partnerships: technology and its application in real estate. In this search for a technology partner, I endeavoured to identify someone who was not just there to make money from hardware sales but was committed to creating a win-win situation with asset owners, to creating value through solutions. By enabling such win-win scenarios, technology solution providers can truly cement their place and emerge as important partners for asset owners and FM services / solution providers.

I have travelled across geographies – Europe, the USA and established IT markets like India – to find a technology solution with a proven track record of enabling efficiency and transformation in megaprojects. After various unsuccessful attempts to find the ideal solution to manage the huge scale of megaprojects, I have formulated a strategy for technology in such megaprojects. This strategy goes beyond Dubai to cover the type of megaprojects emerging across the UAE and the Middle East region. As part of this effort, I established a boutique FM consulting and advisory firm that has worked with megaprojects in Oman, Kuwait, Qatar, Saudi Arabia and the UAE.

As we implemented advisory solutions, we realised that most megaprojects were applying only certain parts of an overall

FM strategy, while missing out on some critical aspects. These omitted aspects invariably included change management, stakeholder education and the evolution, application of technology. The attitude of not wanting to change the way something is done is what holds the FM industry back. This is what stops megaprojects from becoming sustainable as soon as possible and ultimately protecting future megaprojects from making similar mistakes.

This is one aspect that has been important to all of us as FM industry leaders. At MEFMA, we aim to multiply and grow the magnitude of FM impact and make people believe in the transformative power of FM as well as the impact it can bring to megaprojects.

By remembering the words of my wise senior from the first assignment at each stage, I have ensured that I understand the criticality of each of my roles. This is what has helped me enjoy working for diverse portfolios. But this is also where I feel the industry will need to have not just a leader, but multiple leaders and a leadership culture. My work reflects the impact I seek to create in the various organisations I worked with, whether through full-time employment, Phi Strategic Consultancy (my advisory firm), or industry forums such as MEFMA and Global FM.

CHAPTER 4

ENABLING SUSTAINABILITY IN YOUR PROJECT

Making Built Environments Ecological Assets

Let me not mince words about this one strong opinion I hold: sustainability has to be the core pillar (and not just one of the key pillars) of all modern developments in general and megaprojects and beyond in particular. The dictionary definition of "sustainability" is an adjective that stands for "being able to continue over a period of time". However, the term "sustainability" is increasingly being considered as synonymous with its prefixed description of "environmental (or "ecological") sustainability". The impact of environmental sustainability goes well beyond just these definitions. A real estate development can be "sustainable" commercially and from a long-term TCO perspective if it addresses the other definition of the term: "causing, or made in a way that causes, little or no damage to the environment and therefore able to continue for a long time".

This assertion isn't very far-fetched. Take an area like energy management for example. While they vary based on source energy costs from one geography to another, energy / utility costs are 30-40% of total facility running costs in a typical building. Energy management is also a key determinant of a building's carbon footprint. By rationalising energy management, asset owners can realise the dual benefits of rationalised operating expenses (and, by extension, TCO and return on investment of the asset) and contribution to reduced carbon footprint.

The building, as I said, is a living organism. And, like any other organism, its "respiration" is a contributor to the release of carbon into the environment. Is this too absurd an analogy? Are we painting a much grimmer picture of the impact buildings have on the environment than deserved?

Here's an insight to put this in perspective: Edward Mazria is an American architect and the founder of a think tank called Architecture 2030 which promotes thinking on new-age approaches, to minimise the ecological impact of buildings. There are three points of view presented by Mazria that indicate the scale of ecological impact from buildings:

a. In the United States, it is estimated that buildings account for as much as 48% of all greenhouse gas emissions.
b. 40% of this total consumption can be attributed just to building operations. That's heating, lighting, cooling, and hot water.
c. Some larger developments (or what he calls "Oversized Footprint Buildings") have a disproportionately higher ecological impact. The example he gives is from New

York City, where "only 2% of buildings are larger than 50,000 square feet, yet this small percentage is responsible for nearly half of the city's carbon emissions". This is an important statistic in the context of designing megaprojects to support the world's sustainability agenda.

As the above indicates (and there are many other examples of such statistics from across the world), this thought process is now a globally shared area of concern for leaders in the built environment space, from master planners and designers to facility operators and asset managers. If we want to leave a thriving planet for generations to come, sustainability in buildings is a major component we must address.

Throughout my FM career, I have approached sustainability not as an added cost, but as the core enabler of smart living. Unfortunately, we keep missing opportunities to make projects sustainable. We continue rushing the design and construction stages, especially in their planning and final construction milestone, which is the handover to operations determined by a "project handover certificate". In this context, I prefer to use another term: "project birth certificate (PBC)". The PBC is a crucial document that drives long-term sustainability of a project and is a key step in ensuring that FM can have a greater impact on megaprojects and beyond. We'll delve deeper into the concept of PBC later.

As I continue to work on diverse projects across commercial, infrastructure, logistics, residential, leisure and mixed-use asset classes, my aim is to get more people to support the main objective of the FM profession: solidifying our effect on projects, cities and a country's economy. Therefore, if we direct our attention to megaprojects, we can multiply the impact of FM.

As explained earlier, megaprojects are defined as those that have a design and construction cost of at least half a billion dollars, translating into a TCO exceeding USD 2 billion. However, I have seen megaprojects that have been developed over ten years at a cost of USD 25 billion for construction alone. TCO of this scale is not to be taken lightly, and such projects require early-stage involvement of FM expertise, right from the planning and design stage through to construction and handover to operations.

This is where my role in the industry is not to just revitalise existing projects but to push, proactively engage and encourage asset owners to protect future projects by learning from FM experts who are managing projects currently. Implementing an active feedback loop with consultants and other stakeholders is critical to improving and making the design more sustainable and fit for purpose. The consequent scope of FM knowledge value addition across the project lifecycle, especially at the design and build stage is as encapsulated overleaf.

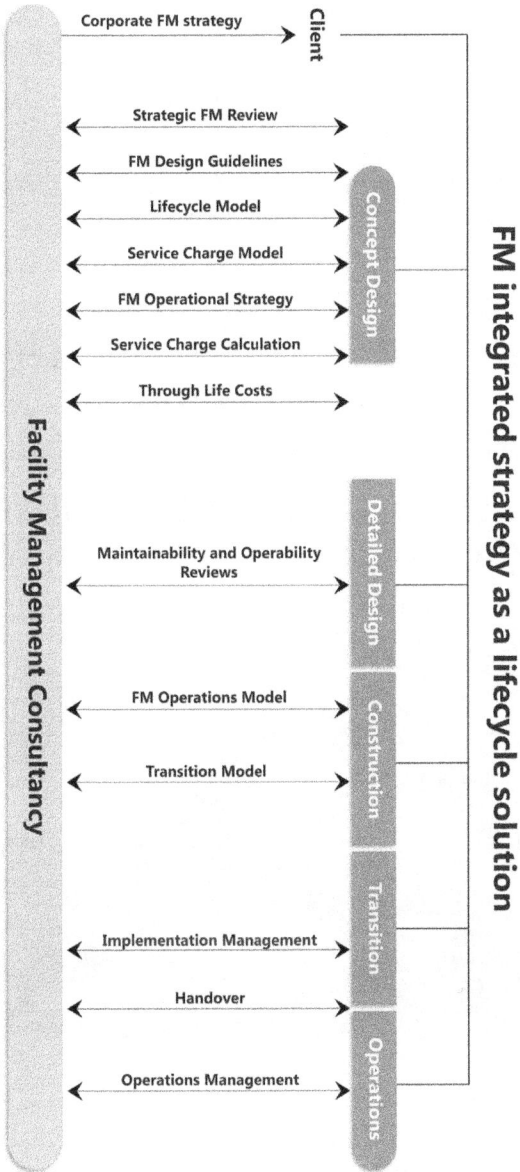

Corporate FM strategy → **Client**

Strategic FM Review

FM Design Guidelines

Lifecycle Model

Service Charge Model

FM Operational Strategy

Service Charge Calculation

Through Life Costs

Concept Design

Maintainability and Operability Reviews

Detailed Design

FM Operations Model

Transition Model

Construction

Implementation Management

Handover

Transition

Operations Management

Operations

Facility Management Consultancy

FM integrated strategy as a lifecycle solution

It is mainly as a result of this belief and approach that my role in the industry has grown gradually, and become critical for asset owners, from government to private sectors, on megaprojects. In my role within MEFMA, I have driven diverse initiatives to convince more people that FM best practices will propel sustainability in megaprojects and beyond. In this regard, one very successful outreach has been a roadshow-style workshop with different megaprojects to discuss the importance of FM and related strategies for handover.

CASE IN POINT: KING ABDULLAH FINANCIAL DISTRICT, SAUDI ARABIA

Saudi Arabia's King Abdullah Financial District (KAFD) in Riyadh is the first mega mixed-use development in the city, spread across 1.6 million square metres of land area with ninety-five buildings, including sixty-four towers designed by twenty-five architects to provide a sustainable and dynamic environment. KAFD received the Leadership in Energy and Environmental Design (LEED) ND Stage 2 Platinum certification, becoming the largest mixed-use financial centre in the world in 2020 to achieve the highest possible accreditation from the world's leading authority for green buildings.[1]

While the project was announced in 2008, this workshop I conducted happened in 2014. From the initial designs in the early 2000s, to actualising King Abdullah's vision, and the start of project construction almost fifteen years ago (now almost completed), the project of this scale and size will benefit immensely from its focus on sustainability and thus aid society. I believe that a strong FM strategy has played a key role in the project achieving its USGBC recognition status.

KAFD is a great example of how FM as best practice should be embedded into the many lifecycle stages and activities such as concept, initial design, detailed design and construction, until it reaches the project birth certificate stage. This needs to be applied to all of the various buildings within the megaproject and infrastructure that form part of these developments, i.e., not just for the master plan.

---

1   Project image and description courtesy of King Abdullah Financial District.

USERS AT THE HEART OF ALL PLANNING

At each of these stages, it is important to keep the customer journey in mind as an important cornerstone. When we design a project, we ensure that the complete project birth certificate process is established and agreed upon by all stakeholders. As part of the strategy, we engage the FM practice as early as the design stage. We embed long-term thinking and then move to position the project as sustainable, taking decisions based on data and operational facts that should be considered at each stage.

ANOTHER KEY STEP IS EMBEDDING TECHNOLOGY INTO THE DATA-GATHERING MECHANISM. THIS IS WHERE I USE A CONCEPT CALLED "THE PILOT ROOM".

In 2009, I was at a crossroads in my career and eager to devise new ways, to put form to my desire to do something truly high impact. It was an interesting inflection point for me. By working with a leading FM service provider, I had already enabled transformation for some of the UAE's largest developments. However, the desire to drive true transformation from within as an asset owner's representative was playing on my mind.

As I usually do during such moments of introspection, I remember sitting in my parked car and looking contemplatively at a skyline dotted with tall towers that were defining the new Dubai – some already built and others under construction.

Amongst those engineering marvels I was looking at, was the most awe-inspiring of them all, the Burj Khalifa, which exemplifies the city's spirit of innovation, enterprise and commitment to global thought leadership. It is providential in this context that the very structure I was looking at created the opportunity for the next level of impact through FM. I had the privilege of being handpicked from the pool of very talented young FM professionals in the nation to be the operations lead for the project.

On my first day at the assignment in July 2009, I saw what emerged as my primary responsibility: Burj Khalifa is like an aeroplane, with a small part on the ground and the rest in the sky. It is a city in itself, albeit vertical! When you need to control something that far up in the sky, you need to empower the teams that drive it with the ability to monitor a complex ecosystem of assets. In order to do this, I established the concept of the FM and Operations Pilot Room, set up like an aeroplane cockpit. Much like how the instrumentation panels in a cockpit are designed, to give the pilot complete visibility into the real-time performance of all critical systems. We designed the operations control room at the Burj Khalifa to enable continuous status update views of critical systems and pre-alarm parameters to minimise disruption in buildings operations. The objective was to proactively ensure efficacy and the health and safety of occupants, similar to the key criteria kept in mind for passengers in an aeroplane. By tracking these parameters, we were also able to rationalise operations and create efficiency to enable sustainable FM operations.

The megaproject, in the context of such pilot rooms, is a series of interconnected smaller projects. Applying the pilot room concept to megaprojects needs to be driven by one parent pilot room for the entire project, with independent component project rooms for each unit – whether a building or a set of floors in a tall building. We need to ensure that we connect all buildings and infrastructure systems, collect data in a data lake set up, and use technology for data analysis to draw smart insights from performance data.

Once developed and proven with the Burj Khalifa, I have promoted this concept as an important mandate for myself in my role as someone who leads the visioning process in the FM industry across the Middle East region and worldwide. I have conducted workshops on implementing the pilot room concept for a variety of megaprojects, including the King Abdullah Financial District. Other megaprojects where I promoted this concept through workshops include the new terminal at the Abu Dhabi Airport and Oman Airport.

THE IDEAL STAGE TO ENGAGE AN FM CONSULTANT

While I thought I was very clear in delivering my message, I did face a wide variety of challenges. Sometimes, the challenge was about not having a structured operating model for when the development would be completed. But mostly it was about FM specialists being included late in project execution, usually at the construction stage. And these situations are indicators of the need to time the involvement of FM strategy with great specificity.

An FM consultant coming in at a stage where they are not able to drive effective communications with all stakeholders of a project (investors, project owners, design consultants and contractors in particular), will result in a loss of valuable inputs to drive operations strategy from early stages. I have seen this happen even at megaprojects. While it is commendable that FM consultants are engaged to provide their insights, it typically happens late in the process. I have also seen the resultant impact of post-facto corrections to adjust design parameters for better operational efficiency – this costs an average of 10% of project cost, let alone the time spent in course corrections.

As industry leaders, we have been emphasising the importance of early FM consultant involvement on projects where the design and construction costs run into several billions of dollars. In such projects, late implementation of FM insights implies that we are only able to partially achieve results and impact.

CASE IN POINT: CITY OF ST. LOUIS, MISSOURI

My work with FM industry associations has exposed me to projects from around the world. One great example of FM planning that I have seen in this context is when I visited St. Louis, Missouri in 2008. During this trip, I realised that I was talking to people who understand the pain of inefficient operations and are trying to achieve outcomes by looking at the different objectives through FM best practices. They have found the answer in technology. During my visit, I saw how data from 830 government buildings and facilities was gathered on design, construction, handover, customer journeys, user profile, user satisfaction testing and long-term impact through sustainability. The focus on sustainability here was not just on saving energy but reducing operational costs, as well as embedding technology and creating the pilot room to move towards centralizing the data of 800-plus buildings.

Today, the city has a total of 3,300 interconnected buildings! This is a stellar example of long-term thinking, and they have done an amazing job of applying what I was looking at in my vision of establishing technology-based FM control centres. Their four-year target was to validate the whole process and improve the role of technology in analysing data to help FM managers further improve the efficacy of FM practices used in their buildings. Of course, now the treasure trove of information is not just used in improving existing buildings, but also to improve designs of future buildings that are similar in nature and intent. With this, buildings can be improved through the feedback rule of understanding the behaviour and challenges of existing design.

THE EIGHT PILLARS OF EXCELLENCE IN FM

Given my involvement in industry associations, one critical value-add to the industry is showcasing the impact of FM best practices on a country's economy through sustainable developments. This has not been an easy task, but my colleagues and I have aimed to change the mindset of diverse stakeholders. This has been the intent through my twelve-year journey with non-profit associations such as MEFMA and Global FM, the umbrella association for FM organisations and professionals in the Middle East and worldwide respectively. This is very important for me – showcasing the big picture is an integral step in stemming inefficient design practices and improving the quality of life for users.

Based on my observations through this process, I believe there are **eight pillars of achieving Impactful FM** in megaprojects and beyond.

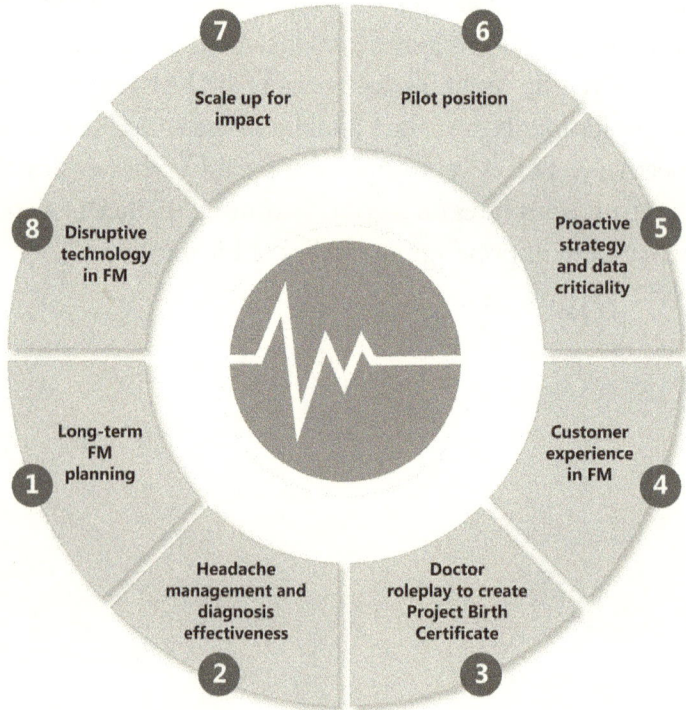

Through the next eight chapters of this book, I will cover these pillars that form the foundation of achieving Impactful FM. These pillars can be applied to all lifecycle stages of any megaproject. For example, at the operations stage, we need to look at design criteria and how design is enabling a seamless customer journey. Or how design is increasing operation and energy costs and what we can do to improve in this context.

Therefore, all of us need to establish long-term thinking and assess the design, testing and commissioning activities at the handover stage. This will ensure we have clarity on system and user profiles, as well as aspects such as weather conditions, which play an important role in maintenance and energy practices. For example, if you frequently have dusty weather conditions, maintenance and cleaning needs are going to be higher than usual. If you don't perform regular maintenance, you'll likely have an increased cost of energy. These are all examples of how data collection, data analysis and embedding, integrating technology play important roles in enabling impactful FM.

The St. Louis case is a very clear indicator of success in using technology to your advantage. Dubai Silicon Oasis is another great example of perfection in megaproject master planning.

CASE IN POINT: DUBAI SILICON OASIS

The government of Dubai owns the master plan for Dubai Silicon Oasis. This plan puts the headquarters of the Dubai Silicon Oasis Free Zone in the middle, with residential, commercial and retail clusters around it. Other infrastructure surrounding the headquarters includes community spaces, schools and hospitals, effectively creating a mini city that operates to very high levels of sustainability.

Sustainable developments are achieved by integrating all infrastructure and developed assets to ensure a superior quality of life for the user. This is where the eight pillars of Impactful FM are important to apply. Transformation through technology and artificial intelligence (AI) use – such as detection rule setting with subject matter experts – helps predict failure and achieve higher effectiveness. Fault detection mechanisms help react to certain parameters for systems, avoiding failure of these systems.

All in all, Dubai Silicon Oasis is a great example of using principles of sound master planning and deep technology integration to facilitate large sustainable communities.

DON'T WAIT FOR THE COMPLAINTS!

The other important aspect to address here is the customer experience. We should not be waiting for customers to complain, but approach problem-solving based on different parameters that emerge as per fault detection rules. For example, if the weather is dusty, the filter will be frequently choked with dust, leading to the failure of air-conditioning systems. Systems will not wait for the next scheduled preventative maintenance. Therefore, by monitoring the condition and pressure of filters for this air conditioning unit, you can send a technician to clean them before they fail. You can also use such data insights to take actions like reducing air intake from fresh air or shutting it down with conditions to reduce faults, and maintenance and energy costs. Practices of this nature also need to be designed carefully. In this example of air conditioning filters, it is best practice that air intake reduction or shutdown be done for just a few hours especially if the dusty weather condition is over the weekend when employees are not in their offices.

Therefore, it is important for all of us to think about these eight pillars of FM strategy, as certain pillars will be important to embed into the design where possible. Come to think of it, the first pillar of long-term FM thinking and planning encompasses all seven pillars that follow. Ultimately, it has to be calibrated and verified during the operational stage, but it should ideally be implemented during the construction stage and commissioned during the handover and building birth or project birth certificate stage. For existing mega and giga projects, this is even more critical and it is worth redoing the technology integration, looking at the customer journey and design criteria for the building so you can have a better impact – even if not this has not been included at the design stage.

The pillars of Impactful FM are truly interlinked, and you have to work on all eight of them together for the effect to be maximised. They are like a chain that simultaneously links up to long-term thinking and forming critical paths. Setting data rules using technology to analyse data can be completed at once to form this critical path. In addition, it is important to look at the customer journey to improve design, energy and maintenance costs. Doing so will result in more effective mega and giga projects that will improve various aspects of the project itself, benefit different business sectors such as schools, hospitals, hotels, residential and commercial, and improve the overall economy of the city and country. We will become more sustainable on environmental, social and economic aspects if Impactful FM strategies are implemented correctly.

That final point is the main takeaway of this chapter. We need to talk about the impact of FM on mega and giga projects. From an industry perspective, we must be more proactive in discussing these best practices and how we can link them together to optimise benefits from a sustainability perspective. This is an important element for all of us, and it is essential to remember that "we shape our buildings; thereafter they shape us". (Winston Churchill)

It is vital that we clearly communicate what we need to do to harness this impact.

CHAPTER 5

PILLAR 1: LONG-TERM THINKING

The Criticality of Understanding Long-Term Commitments for Megaprojects

The UAE I grew up in was all about unwavering focus and intent to emerge as a strong nation. Our nation's founding fathers had a clear vision for the future of our country as a beacon for the world to follow. The UAE of today that the entire world sees is a glittering example of success, vibrancy and innovation.

Through sheer determination and perseverance, previous generations have established and propelled this country forward, transforming it into the global force for excellence and innovation that it is today. We were taught from an early age that everything we do has a larger purpose and that our actions have a role in building something bigger than us.

This long-term thinking has now been woven into the philosophy of our citizens – from our leaders to the people who drive the wheels of our great economic and technological progress.

In 2016, His Highness Sheikh Mohammed bin Rashid Al Maktoum, ruler of Dubai and the Vice President and Prime Minister of UAE gifted us with a symbol that put form to this spirit of the UAE. This symbol is the three-finger salute that stands for Win, Victory and Love.

You see me here, with the three-finger salute while on top of the Burj Khalifa, the most appropriate symbol of these three qualities that have shaped the UAE. Megaprojects are no different because it is only when you pour the labour of love into every aspect of a megaproject that you create magic. And this labour of love starts with an eye for detail from the very first stage of planning.

DESIGN RIGHT. BUILD RIGHT. OPERATE RIGHT.

In this chapter, I highlight the importance of long-term thinking and how FM planning can be introduced in a megaproject from the concept design stage. This is critical as it helps set up the plan for achieving environmental and financial sustainability while maximising FM impact. This long-term thinking is all about **designing** right, **building** right and **operating** right. These three components of design, build and operation are seamlessly entwined in the FM strategy, which is a true reflection of long-term thinking.

We all know this. Why then do we fail to walk the talk? Why do we lose focus on long-term thinking in megaprojects? Several factors limit long-term thinking and lifecycle assessment during the early stages of concept and strategy setting in a megaproject. One of these factors is limited time and the challenges faced in achieving targets related to design and construction stage completion. Another factor is the existence of very little information about end-user requirements and project operational strategy for megaprojects. Long-term thinking is the first and most important pillar to formulate an impactful FM strategy. This requires more planning than ever before.

FAILING TO PLAN IS PLANNING TO FAIL

Long-term thinking is all about learning from existing projects and ascertaining current gaps and mistakes made in similar developments. During the planning stage, we need to evaluate similar projects and listen to users of these facilities to achieve better lifecycle costing and related assessment for future megaprojects. As a result, we can improve the efficiency of our investment in different sectors, including education, healthcare, residential, commercial, retail, and infrastructure assets. This is where long-term thinking and related feedback loops are critical.

Information gathering is another important element when it comes to planning. Visiting similar existing buildings allows us to look for information that makes new projects more fit for purpose. Let me give you an example: we continue to see mistakes repeated across new school projects, resulting in wasted resources since lighting and air-conditioning designs do not meet school operating requirements and patterns. Another example is higher cost of replacement due to operability and maintainability challenges – this is evident in elevator installations for tall buildings where tension rods have a shorter lifespan and need to be replaced earlier than usual due to design issues. This is critical to avoid elevator entrapment situations. It is clear that we need to see how long it will take to replace equipment or even small assets like lights versus the cost of spare parts and labour. Maintainability and operability aspects of building design are very important in controlling lifecycle costs.

The second crucial aspect of long-term thinking relates to validation of project purpose. FM subject matter experts need to be involved to validate the purpose of the project and establish lifecycle assessment and related costs in that context. The involvement of an FM consultant is needed during concept development and then at the detailed design stage. This will guarantee that operational investment is considered and the total cost of ownership validated while ensuring we embed technology-based FM solutions as part of a long-term thinking philosophy.

Long-term thinking is not just about looking at the first year's requirements as a short-term plan but also making the building sustainable. This involves placing a higher dependence on technology to enable longer-term benefits; for example, digitising the building to monitor and retrieve information that will help with proactive decision-making. Data-based decision-making is very important in the modern era of FM. Without a detailed analysis of design parameter impact on operations, long-term thinking will not have a clear path to success. For example, if you install lights in a hotel's 5-metre-high atrium lobby ceiling, you need to look at the cost of bulb replacement because you will need to rent a high-access machine for this task. It may be better to provide above-ceiling access to do the replacement while examining the cost of both access and operations over the life of the building.

Another example is the performance of the HVAC (heating, ventilation and air-conditioning) system – is it within design criteria to provide optimum cooling and effectively manage energy bills while ensuring lifecycle costs are minimised? In this case, selecting and sizing the various systems is critical.

Without FM consultants who bring in the operational experience from similar projects, it becomes challenging to validate total cost of ownership. As a result, employing an FM expert during the concept design and detailed design stages is a critical component of long-term thinking with technology as a tool to validate. We need to embed technology to validate design behaviour during operations; and this is the feedback loop that must be included in the long-term thinking. Once we have the technology, we can capture data that helps us improve design going forward. Also, long-term thinking helps reduce stress on the operations budget of government and private megaprojects, since oversized infrastructure and inefficient operations of such projects puts a tremendous amount of stress on the financial credibility of government and privately owned corporations.

Finally, long-term thinking enables a proactive approach towards sustainability, by increasing the opportunity for reuse and recycling and eliminating the need for extensive redesign. We need to minimise use and recycle to reduce. We need to conceive and build sustainable megaprojects. This is clearly a result of long-term planning and the design-for-purpose approach that I recommend, followed by embedding technology to measure and collect data. FM subject matter experts assist in the design, analysis and validation of purpose and the long-term roadmap, of which sustainability is again a result.

Long-term thinking is the only way we can be successful in megaprojects moving forward, and we need to ensure that this is a natural step in the process. We must revisit existing megaproject cases and learn from them, especially in mixed-use developments that are built in half the time it usually takes. Capturing such operational thinking at the planning stage helps address challenges early on.

I have several stories and examples that illustrate the pitfalls of avoiding long-term thinking and the huge impact this can have on quality and cost. Eventually, these two elements impact the sustainability and financial success of megaprojects.

Long-term thinking should be made a culture. This will help us make the right decisions at early stages of the project lifecycle and understand the total cost of ownership of the megaproject, rather than just the initial cost. The more insights that drive it, the better a decision is, which is a true reflection of long-term thinking.

There is an obvious need to consider current challenges in existing projects and how they can be tackled. This is what we are going to explore in the next chapter, where we talk about handling existing projects, especially at the handover stage.

CHAPTER 6

PILLAR 2: FM OPERATIONAL DIAGNOSIS EFFECTIVENESS: HEADACHE MANAGEMENT

The Importance of Spotting Issues and Having Short- and Long-Term Solutions during the First Year of Operation (Post-Occupancy) Once Beneficial Occupancy Starts

Imagine you rush the decision to move into a new mixed-use development where you will be using the various occupancy facilities such as residential, offices, amenities (swimming pool, gym, among others), restaurants, parking, etc. Now imagine living with the post-occupancy challenges of a community whose construction work is not complete and major snags are not fully attended to within the common area and the various occupancy use zones. This scenario is, unfortunately, quite common in the first occupancy year of most projects in the Middle East region, especially in megaprojects. This occurs when we rush the transition and the move from the construction stage to operational.

UNDERSTANDING BENEFICIAL OCCUPANCY AND NUANCES WITHIN IT

"Beneficial occupancy" describes a real estate asset that can be used for its intended purpose while still awaiting the resolution of (minor) defects. In reality, it has started to be misconstrued as starting to use a building without a complete handover from a construction team to an operational team, where the process of addressing obstacles, testing and commissioning building equipment and assets, and operator training is incomplete. This results in operational challenges and gaps, causing health, safety and discomfort issues for users.

We have already talked in the previous chapter about long-term thinking. In this chapter, we are going to highlight the feedback loop of operational issues that will need to be considered in your long-term thinking process. The intent is to ensure that you develop a post-occupancy strategy to avoid mistakes that happen if you don't implement this process, especially if you do not have a clear handover strategy from project to operation. It is imperative to identify the pain points and develop quick solutions to manage these huge projects. We have a lot of headaches and pain areas while managing megaprojects during handover and post-occupancy stages.

So, what are these mistakes and why do we keep making them repeatedly?

Once projects become operational, the headache and pain points are very high. As a result, you need to have a strategy to observe, identify and find short- and long-term solutions for these pain points that affect user experience and building efficiency. You have to track the demand of the facility versus services that have been provided. For example, FM strategy may dictate the need for a service level agreement to clean the external window on monthly basis. However, design limitations may imply that the building maintenance unit (BMU) can only do one full cycle every three months.

In addition, construction and building design-related risks might suddenly trigger various pain points, such as overcooling in certain spots among other issues, once the various buildings become operational. You need to identify these weak spots and manage them.

By end of this chapter, you will realise that gaps in design, construction and handover of projects are often repeated. As a result, you need a strategy for headache and pain identification, and solutions to overcome these challenges. In addition, you need to be able to understand what is happening in these megaprojects and design short- and long-term solutions. This is how we can lead by example in managing occupant and functional issues once megaprojects become operational.

UNDERSTANDING WHAT IS HAPPENING

We need to understand that all megaprojects have various gaps to manage once they are operational. What if we can identify and manage them to ensure we optimise our resources and improve customer experience? What is stopping us from doing this effectively? We keep missing such opportunities until the issue becomes critical or it's simply too late to resolve. What is happening in any megaproject or even a smaller-sized project once it is operational?

You need to have a plan to be healthy and to stay healthy. The same concept is critical in these huge projects. Most of the time, this is unfortunately not the case when it comes to megaprojects in our region (and worldwide). Increasingly, we are seeing a greater sense of urgency to open and operate the project even if it is not ready (or what we introduced earlier as "beneficial occupancy"). Frequently recurring gaps appear with improper testing and commissioning, and insufficient project information shared between construction / project teams and operations teams. Outlined below are example pain points which occur most often that we should look at avoiding in future projects.

SHORT-TERM SOLUTIONS

We currently only consider short-term solutions rather than having clear long-term solutions to tackle issues and related operational requirements. Therefore, if there is a challenge or a gap affecting the operation of this project, we primarily look at short-term solutions and rush to find the most appropriate answer to plug the leak rather than addressing source issues. For example, if the AC is not cooling, we add extra units rather than understanding the root of the issue and how it can be resolved for the long term. It's imperative that we properly diagnose the gap and put forward short and long-term solutions that will enhance effectiveness of operations and improve user experience.

We need to understand current project gaps and undertake the required diagnosis. This is critical to tackle pain points and improve safety measures and end-user satisfaction. Design and operational requirements – including risk assessment – need to be performed by subject matter experts. This is why we need to understand during the early stage of handover where obstacles may arise. Some issues might continue as chronic problems (repeated every year) if it not solved permanently.

We have many examples of projects that missed the opportunity to have a healthy operation and user experience because they did not manage critical data transfer from construction stakeholders to operation stakeholders. One example I often detect in projects of all scales is the testing and commissioning of water systems and ensuring proper system flushing.

It is evident from the above that there is a fundamental problem when it comes to project overlap between the construction and operation stages. One of the main issues is integration between these two stages, especially in megaprojects where we miss opportunities to implement the right strategy from the beginning.

While working with a large FM services company, I remember an instance where a water pump failed in a villa occupied by a VIP in a large prestigious project for which we were in the process of assuming operations. I received a call that the pump was under warranty and the contractor would need at least forty-eight hours to organise a replacement. I saw no clear responsibility matrix with a clearly stated response time to address this situation. As a solution, I got the team to start supplying fresh water directly to the tank, adding a redundant pump until the water pump issue was solved.

These are examples of issues that were presented during the handover and which, without proper attention, would affect user experience and lifespan, efficacy of various facilities.

HIDDEN RISKS OF POOR DIAGNOSIS

Megaprojects are subject to mega risks, and the most dangerous ones are those that are hidden. Imagine the risk associated with water flooding in an electrical room or elevator shaft where the probability of the main water line (water shaft) being in close proximity to critical electrical systems is high – a recipe for disaster. One of the first steps in planning operations for a megaproject is the creation of a risk register.

Risk register development is an important process and needs to be implemented as early as the testing and commissioning stage. There is no perfect design system for any megaproject. There will be limitations and the idea is to ensure that we diagnose the problem and manage this pain area. This will always appear in the first year of operation and there is an opportunity for all of us to go back and monitor through data collected in the first year of operation to build a culture of continuous improvement.

This will help ensure that we have a clear identification of risks and challenges. This will also enable the required short and long-term adjustment to ensure that facilities at megaprojects and different buildings within it are effectively managed, resources are optimised and energy consumption is efficient.

STAKEHOLDER RESPONSIBILITY MATRICES

It is important to have clear role descriptions so each resource does their part (stakeholders role) in the transition from construction to operations. The identification of stakeholder roles will help the operations team be proactive. In this context, it's not just the FM consultant role that is important, but also that of the design consultant for different systems. Further, it is important to have the right testing and commissioning strategy with appropriate resources. A systems designer needs to be involved during the first year to monitor and examine the behaviour of various systems and the building's usage pattern. This will ensure that we identify and adjust deficiencies to improve the function of building facilities.

Various stakeholders are involved in the first year of operation because this stage is key in any project. This is why the main objective of this chapter is to highlight as many regularly occurring pain points as possible. One of the major pain points is the increased cost of operation because of flaws related to accessibility. This is clear in many projects where, for example, the waste truck cannot enter the facility because the vehicle clearance isn't high enough. As a result, waste bins have to be manually pushed from the basement to the ground floor – an obvious operational pain point.

Another operational pain point is the single point of failure in water networks. I had the experience of having six G+10 high-end buildings which were connected to the same water tank. So, failure in the outgoing pipe from the tank implied no water supply in all six buildings at the same time. This could be avoided by analysing the risk and ensuring redundancy and reliability through monitoring of water pressure in pipes to avoid the unpleasant situation of having no water in buildings housing 20,000+ residents – a clear example of a design flaw that caused major operational impact.

I'd like to provide another example of a "solution" to an operational issue that only created a larger issue: foul smell in an office space when the waste management room extract was switched on. To stop the smell permeating the office area, the FM team kept the waste room extract fan off which caused hygiene problems and health issues for the waste room maintenance team. When we visited the site as FM consultants with operational backgrounds, we noticed the smell in the waste room and questioned why the extract fans were kept off. We immediately identified the gap in design: an extract fan exhaust on the roof that was in close proximity to the office's fresh air system. The permanent solution was to keep both the extract and the fresh air system far from each other on the roof.

These are some simple examples of issues that you will encounter if you don't study the handover stage in detail and manage risks proactively. Risk assessment has to be based on different applications or utilisation of the building compared to the design element. Also, sometimes design elements have limitations due to restricted space. For example, to have seven tanks for several buildings or one-plus-one for each building, we may have space limitations. This is where the single point of failure might immediately affect the operation of these towers as the aim of design is to save common services space, which negatively impacts customer experience and attractiveness of residential communities in the long term.

LEADING BY EXAMPLE

You need to lead by example and become proactive. For example, having as-built drawings and documentation that will enable the operation team to operate and maintain the health of different systems is a crucial element of any handover. This is one of the headaches and the pain points we see worldwide – when the building has been almost completed, we miss optimization opportunities since we have limited paperwork. Completion of such by construction stakeholders leads to the handover being delayed until the first year of operation rather than happening during three months before the operation stage, which is ideal.

To address this, we urge stakeholders to work in close coordination as early as one year before handover, ensuring that we have the appropriate accountable operations experts looking at the various systems, understanding how to commission them, test them and make them ready for operation. We can optimise all opportunities, especially in giga projects, as these projects represent a major part of modern cities.

I have worked with various developers who lead by example to ensure that they always identify pain points and manage the headaches that emerge in the first few months or first year of operation. Documenting issues, ensuring they have qualified people on the ground who understand the system, addressing the requirement or adjusting settings, and effectively managing the building will guarantee a top-tier customer experience.

This is what we need to do to lead by example. But since long-term solutions often take longer to achieve, we must also consider short-term solutions. This is where the collaboration between construction stakeholders, the consultant, the main contractor, electrical, mechanical and plumbing contractors, the civil subcontractor and specialised subcontractors plays a key role. There must also be a collaboration between these bodies, the FM company in charge of handover and the owner representative. Doing this ensures the right strategy can be put in place to identify pain points that occur in the first few months, particularly during periods of extreme weather.

The primary pain point you will encounter is snags related to engineering – mechanical, electrical, plumbing and civil. This is where condition assessment is not just a role of the FM professional but a joint effort and collaboration between the different stakeholders. This is what we call recommissioning. Together, all the stakeholders must plan, investigate and action recommendations during the first year and verification phase.

This illustration overleaf reflects the critical roles of different stakeholders.

Stakeholder involvement

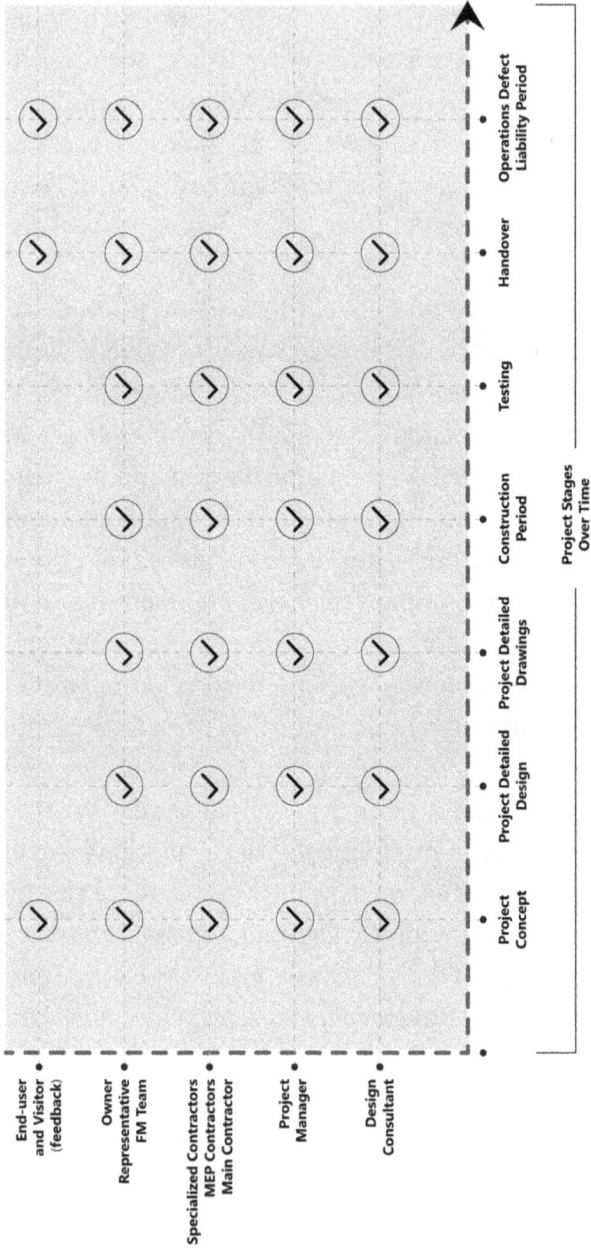

	Project Concept	Project Detailed Design	Project Detailed Drawings	Construction Period	Testing	Handover	Operations Defect Liability Period
End-user and Visitor (feedback)							
Owner Representative FM Team							
Specialized Contractors MEP Contractors Main Contractor							
Project Manager							
Design Consultant							

Project Stages Over Time

It is during this early stage of operation that FM and technology usage will help identify and manage FM operations, adjusting to the end-user requirement. It is also at this stage that we can ensure systems are recommissioned to fit the purpose and objective of users, while striving for sustainability. This will help further our agenda of FM having greater impact on sustainability in megaprojects.

Dubai Silicon Oasis is a powerful example of effective pain point management in megaprojects. Like any other megaproject, not everything in this development worked perfectly during the handover. However, from the handover stage itself, there was a strategy and attention to detail that helped it emerge as an attractive megaproject destination. It is a huge master plan, comprising commercial buildings, residences, hospitals, malls and a school, all of which were handed over correctly, with risk registers in place and a structured process for identification and rectification of snags, thereby tackling all related pain points.

Ultimately, this is a clear example of leadership that effectively helps resolve complications. Interlinked with long-term thinking, this prioritisation and attention to the first year of operation lay the foundation for doctor involvement during the early stages. The next pillar we will cover is the approach of building birth certificates rather than handover certificates.

CHAPTER 7

PILLAR 3: DOCTOR ROLE-PLAY TO CREATE PROJECT BIRTH CERTIFICATE

Getting the Right Operational Start

You see pictures of the new Dubai – tall skyscrapers that dot our skyline. Most of these are images from Sheikh Zayed Road, the arterial road around which most of modern Dubai has been developed. The road itself isn't new – it has been the highway that connects Abu Dhabi and Dubai for a long time now. But my intent is not to deliver a lecture on geography. An iconic image from the early 1990s shows the view from the top of the Emirates Towers, one of the earliest high-rise developments in Dubai. On a clear day like the one on which this picture was taken, you can see Dubai with mostly low-rise commercial buildings and housing, all the way up to what is today the fourth interchange on Sheikh Zayed Road: a distance of almost 8-10 kilometres as the crow flies from Emirates Towers.

To me, this photograph is an iconic representation of the progress our nation has made. I was born around the same time that our great nation was founded, and started my career around the time that our great leaders and founding fathers started putting shape to the vision of a new UAE. My career growth, therefore, has run parallel to the growth of the UAE making its mark on the world stage.

WORKING WITH DIVERSE FM PARTNERS

This is true of many of my colleagues in the UAE, as well as those around the region and indeed across the world. I consider the early and mid-2000s as one of the significant inflection points in the field of facility management; many principles of what we consider modern FM were conceptualised in this period. As I have gone through my career growth cycle, one of the key insights that emerged is how FM is as much about engineering as it is about softer aspects such as muscle memory, reflex thinking and instinct. You will not find all the answers to situations faced in everyday operations in engineering manuals. Innovative thinking and a problem-solving approach are integral parts of the FM professional's mental makeup.

In my first assignments in building operations and maintenance, this baffled me a little bit. This is where, fortunate to be guided by very intelligent seniors, I was taught an important professional life lesson that "FM is as much an art as it is a science". Today, twenty-five years later, I have my own version of this expression. I have come to realise how FM encompasses diverse disciplines. One of the core disciplines we tend to overlook is human behaviour. What we call user experience (something I will cover in a later chapter as a key pillar) is, in essence, the art and science of understanding and responding to human expectations from the built environment. A building that doesn't cater to the needs of its occupiers is a collection of concrete, steel and glass; one that does is a living, thriving element of our everyday lives. This is what makes the difference between an ordinary development and a great one.

So, to me, the reading of FM now is that it is a combination of "science, art **and the philosophy that helps understand human behaviour**". I pride myself on being a contemplative person. I like to think through why we do what we do and how we can do it differently to better ourselves and all those we affect.

Therefore, I have looked at the building handover process with the same sense of applying science, art and philosophy. From this philosophical thinking emerged the concept of the building birth certificate. For a majority of the time that human civilisation and settlements have been around, there has been a societal desire to set the context to an individual. We like to capture all essential details that determine a human being's existence, whether it is a simple documentation of details such as parents and generations before or more complex efforts like horoscopes in astrology.

As this system has evolved, capturing a person's information at birth has become much more efficient and comprehensive; almost all of it is captured in a seemingly innocuous document called the birth certificate – a lifelong reference point that captures all details that contextualise our existence as a human being from day one. This being applied to the built environment gave rise to the building birth certificate concept. And, to take the analogy further, it indicated the need for an expert (like the gynaecologist / obstetrician) to ensure that all details are captured accurately and in entirety. In the context of larger developments including megaprojects, the same concept is what I call the **project** birth certificate.

THE SUCCESS OF AN FM SUBJECT MATTER EXPERT IS YOUR SUCCESS

This sentiment is especially true in the case of megaprojects. As I have covered in detail earlier in this book, FM subject matter experts play a critical role and their success in the assignment has a major role to play in the success of the megaproject as a whole.

These subject matter experts are part of the ecosystem that enables a powerful development strategy and, for us (the community of FM professionals), their role is similar to that of a doctor, replete with observation, symptom capture, diagnosis and treatment. These "project doctors" are the critical cogs who drive well-designed project handover strategies.

The additional role I assign to these project doctors is to ensure that a project birth certificate strategy is formulated. This step helps transfer all knowledge from the project stage into the operations stage, which is the longest cycle in a megaproject development lifecycle, accounting for 75%-90% of project time and cost.

The project handover certificate (PHC) is the traditional route followed to get a release on contractor completion of their scope of work. This is usually signed off by a project consultant and endorsed by the owner representative (or project manager if available). The problem here is that a PHC focuses on capturing and certifying – regardless of construction stakeholders meeting their obligations – with very little focus on understanding design risk and operational limitations. All of this typically happens while documentation and testing and commissioning are being rushed and not completely made fit for the project, resulting in loss of complete knowledge transfer between the construction and operations stages.

PROJECT BIRTH CERTIFICATE APPROACH

This new approach helps hand over and transition between construction and operation stages in a way that establishes the right lifecycle strategy, covering aspects such as operability, maintainability and operational approach. Particularly on the latter, executing a project successfully involves a superior operational strategy once detailed drawings are ready, while ensuring we examine the total cost of ownership and lifecycle assessment / lifecycle costing of the project.

All these tasks are completed by the FM subject matter expert. Moreover, most megaprojects are missing a responsibility matrix to manage the overlap between construction and operational stakeholders. Again, this is an assignment that can be effectively performed by the project doctor. One component of the responsibility matrix is defining clarity of roles of both the operators and FM service providers, the scope of main contractor and subcontractors with response time for diverse zones. For example, the response time for the hotel component of a mixed-use complex may have to be faster than others.

REVOLUTIONISING THE HANDOVER PROCESS

We need to change the way handover takes place today. Project handovers across the world happen in a simple way that covers only the consultant contractor's scope and rarely interrogates the validation of operational requirements or total cost of ownership. This is why we need to engage FM consultants with relevant project operational expertise as early as the project concept stage. They can start working closely with design consultants, the construction main contractor, subcontractors and specialised contractors within the construction project phase. They can then move and work with the operational team to ensure that total cost of ownership is validated. This is very important for all megaprojects and beyond.

Normal handover practice – building handover certificate	FM best practice for handover – project birth certificate approach
As-built drawings are submitted late and need validation from the operation team during the first year of operation.	As-built drawings are validated during the final stage before handover by the concerned project consultant and FM consultant and made ready before the project operation date.
Various documentation not submitted on time or missing (e.g., authority approval documents, spare part list, asset register, operation and maintenance manuals, operator training manual, and fire life safety procedure among other emergency evacuations are not fully submitted before day one operation stage). It may take six months to one year to be completed.	Close monthly coordination by all construction stakeholders to prepare these documents and establish a digital library and hardcopy register for all essential operations from day one of project operation.

Normal handover practice – building handover certificate	FM best practice for handover – project birth certificate approach
No full lifecycle assessment and total cost of ownership study is conducted.	Lifecycle assessment and total cost of ownership assessment are done and validated at various construction stages (initial design, detailed design and construction stage).
No risk assessment register is established, as this does not fall under the construction stakeholder's scope.	Review of all potential design and system-related risks and related impact. Establishing of risk register and mitigation plan.
No responsibility matrix is established during the overlap between construction and operation during the first year of the defect liability period, leading to slow response to occupant and operational snags.	A clear responsibility matrix for each stakeholder is established with a definite response time and respective zones within the project.

By the end of this chapter, you will be able to understand how critical it is to have **FM** consultant involvement to set up the roadmap for megaproject lifecycles, thereby improving communication and roles, and the responsibility of different stakeholders. You will also understand why the handover strategy is critical for all projects, and the importance of implementing a birth certificate approach from construction to operational stakeholders through the handover phase rather than the typical handover approach. Clear **FM** consultant role can be summarised on various deliverables during design, detailed design, construction, and transition stage from project to operation stage.

STARTING RIGHT

In addition to my early understanding of the subject, as I visit the new and upcoming iconic projects in the region, I continue to discover critical operational limitations that have the potential to increase the risk and cost of operating a project. For example, through my experiences, I have witnessed the importance of fire detection systems in supertall buildings that form part of a megaproject. The learning here is the need to establish sufficient fire zones per floor to avoid a situation of insufficient fire alarm system coverage, which can happen if one zone is spread across multiple floors. When fit-out activities take place in a unit on a particular floor, fire alarm systems are switched off, since dust from fit-out work can trigger these alarms. Given that a lot of fit-out work happens in the first year of operations, such fire alarm outages can be a major source of risk. The reason for this is the alarm is kept off not just for the area under fit-out but also on a few other floors is due to limitation of fire zones, which may have been done to save cost. The cost of creating more fire zones is well worth it, considering the risk.

By contemplating operational strategy during the concept design of a megaproject, through the involvement of an FM consultant, your project lifecycle starts in the right direction, as all aspects of cost, environmental impact and user requirements are captured. The FM consultant plays an important role by supporting the design process with user experience considerations. This is also kept in context while defining the service scope for the FM company and how lifecycle costing can be minimised, rather than just focusing on construction cost savings.

This is where, to have the right start, we establish a strategy of operation during design and adjust the design to make the operational strategy fit for purpose – whether on sustainability, financial impact, user experience, risk management, efficiency and effectiveness, or the quality of life of users of megaprojects. As a result, the operational commencement is supported by qualified, competent consultants, working closely with the owner, looking at projects of a similar magnitude and integrating services between the different buildings within megaprojects. These factors ensure that there is continuity when it comes to customer experience during development. The operational strategy takes care of minute details – for example, parking designed in a way that offers easy accessibility to buildings, thereby ensuring a good experience for users.

At the same time, we need to look at the operator of these projects (FM and related services) and the megaproject community to develop tools that they can utilise to do their job with safe practices and minimal risk. This must be executed while maintaining the visibility of various systems to ensure that we highlight sustainability benefits like the reduction of energy cost and operational costs.

An important example of the operability of any facility is the use of building a maintenance unit for cleaning glass surfaces. It's important to look at the service level expected from the user of the building, i.e., how frequently we need to clean the glass. We need to look at weather conditions, and then the design of these units. Do we really need a building maintenance unit? How long it will take to clean the windows if we have this building maintenance component? How about looking at options of having hooks that will give people access to clean the window faster with a rope access system? Can we make this arrangement during construction, rather than during the operations stage? This is a typical example of validation of operability and maintainability of different systems and their link to a better experience for building users.

It is important to develop a checklist for sustainability as the "why" of validating the operational strategy during design. There are a lot of elements that are very important for all stakeholders of the built environment and cover the various systems and people experiences. This is why getting the right start is imperative: designing different systems and spaces, and making sure critical systems data is sent to the control room, so operators take proactive measures to effectively manage risks and costs.

This is important when we talk about the right start involving FM consultants and subject matter experts to validate the operational strategy, spare part requirement, accessibility, and customer experience of a megaproject during design.

ROADMAP TO SUCCESS

The second point we discuss in this chapter is the need to ensure that one of the most important enablers of success – a communication plan between the different stakeholders – is put in place. Having the right FM subject matter expert, creating the right scope for the consultant and main contractor during the handover stage, validating the operational strategy during design and detailed design are essential tools that help configure the right roadmap to success when it comes to transitioning between the project and operational stages. For example, many developers make sure that they embed the handover strategy within the consulting and contractor scope. This exercise closes communication gaps. To ensure this, you will need a FM consultant and FM operational representative to be involved as early as at least one year before handover. There is a strong need to establish communication protocols, work openly in a transparent manner to capture challenges and risks and make sure that we are creating long-term operational strategies for megaprojects. The goal is to be proud of our achievements as project stakeholders or operational stakeholders.

I reiterate that the FM consultant (or megaproject doctor as we call them) needs to be involved as early as the concept / design of a project. This is an important step towards establishing a clear communication plan that will help reduce communication gaps during handover and post-handover.

CLARITY OF DRIVE

The third point is the need to ensure clarity of drive through the involvement of strategic and technical FM consultants. The outcome of their involvement includes detailed operational strategies to validate the operability and maintainability of facilities as well as the consideration of end-user requirements.

I believe that the typical handover strategy is not sufficient in megaprojects. We need something more detailed as a reflection of a true handover: the project birth certificate. We need to understand that it's not a simple exercise where we just look at what needs to be delivered versus what is being delivered. The PBC approach involves monitoring the behaviour of the megaproject to ensure that we anticipate risks, because there is no such thing as a one hundred per cent perfect design.

Once we start the most critical stage of handover – testing and commissioning – we need to have different parameters that will enable capture of as much documentation as needed before the consultant and the contractor demobilise from the site.

This is why we call this stage the project birth certificate, and this is part of the clarity of driving objective. Everybody needs to see how important handover is, which in reality should start by engaging an FM consultant from the day you plan a building. This is where we make sure that we have an overlap between the construction and operational stages. We also need to ensure that knowledge about the building is transferred. We can validate with the users of the building whether we are able to meet their objectives. Do we have any gaps in the design that we need to capture and work around?

Accordingly, clarity of the drive is an important part of handover. For example, construction stakeholders such as the project consultant and contractor don't typically focus on spotting design risks, but focus instead on following the design scope of work. This culminates in a big design risk such as locating a water riser above an electrical room. In such situations, there is a major safety risk in case of a leak in the water shaft on the floor just above the electrical room.

Most of the time the handover exercise unfortunately stops once people start using the building. On the other hand, the birth certificate as a handover strategy will continue to be in action during the liability period, which is the first year of operation, where we need the involvement of the consultant and contractor. We put in place a system that helps tackle issues with user experience through the first year and make sure that the megaproject is poised to grow into something sustainable, more efficient and effective (for which we capture all safety risks as well). This is where we need clarity of drive.

Handover liability will continue to be with construction stakeholders even after a project has become operational and until they complete all works. There are many examples of projects that were built very fast where all steps that needed to be taken care of were not addressed effectively. For example, there was no FM consultant. There was no documentation. There was no proper testing and commissioning. The construction stage was also done as a fast-track exercise.

I have seen these gaps being clearly missed in a mall project that was built within a year and where, 15 years later, the asset is not achieving its mission from a commercial and sustainability perspective. This is where it is important for all of us to look at projects, and megaprojects in particular to ensure enough time for design and construction. We involve the lifecycle and total cost of ownership expert – the FM consultant – to validate so we can improve the design and have quality construction and handover. With the involvement of different stakeholders, the right communication is vital for all of us. This is also how we can make sure that we embed technology into projects to monitor critical systems. FM can be a proactive element of success if we involve the doctor (the right FM stakeholder) to prevent, rather than cure, during operation.

In essence, we need a roadmap to be successful in achieving megaproject objectives. We need to have a clear communication plan and set up a megaproject birth certificate strategy to ensure seamless transfer of knowledge and a well-executed operational strategy. We also need to delve deeper into customer experience to achieve the quality of life for all users of the project.

CASE IN POINT: BURJ KHALIFA BIRTH CERTIFICATE STRATEGY IMPLEMENTATION

The FM operations team I led at Burj Khalifa as part of the asset management team successfully implemented the project birth certificate concept developed by me. Various forms were used as best practice, integrated with construction stakeholders and used to collect data to guide the process. As part of implementing the entire process, a risk register comprising various critical systems (wind, electrical, mechanical and water among others) was established. I involved an FM consultant during the design and construction stages to attend design workshops and validate the operability and maintainability of various FM services. A responsibility matrix was introduced and a third-party specialised vendor appointed to oversee the testing and commissioning stage. We ensured the hire and onboarding of a competent operations management team and related FM service providers six months before opening. Involvement of construction stakeholders continued for over two years post going live, especially on aspects related to operations and control centre connectivity to the various building systems.

We were able to successfully, effectively and safely lead the transition of this complex web of interwoven systems that now forms the heart of the world's tallest building. Today, the Burj Khalifa operates at the highest levels of efficiency, user satisfaction and asset dependability. It has emerged as a prestigious development, not just by itself but also in the community that has been built surrounding it. I would like to think that some credit for the building's status today is due to the initial long-term thinking and project birth certificate approach that was employed at conception.

My experiences with leading this process were captured in an interview with Facilities Management Middle East, a leading industry periodical.

CHAPTER 8

PILLAR 4: CUSTOMER EXPERIENCE IN FM

Get the Facility to Fit for Purpose

*"WHATEVER GOOD THINGS WE BUILD
END UP BUILDING US".*

**- JAMES ROHN, AMERICAN ENTREPRENEUR,
AUTHOR AND MOTIVATIONAL SPEAKER**

Buildings are designed for people to live, work and play. They are designed to facilitate the best possible quality of life for them in the context of the use / purpose for which they were designed. As you walk into your office today or walk back home on the walkways of your residential community, take the time to notice the small things that drive your productivity at work or the joys of spending time with your family.

And then remember the words that my supervisor told me: "It's not until it goes away that people realise the value of something that they take for granted". There are so many factors at play that make your experience – whether the delight from built environments or the safety and wellness that come with it – complete. This is why the concept of Impactful FM has customer experience at its core.

In the continued spirit of outlining the philosophy of FM, in addition to the quote above, there are a few other quotes that I find truly inspirational. One of these, which I used earlier in this book, is from Winston Churchill: "We shape our buildings, thereafter they shape us". Another is from the Canadian architect Arthur Erickson: "Great buildings that move the spirit have always been rare. In every case, they are unique, poetic products of the heart".

Monuments and landmarks are always a labour of love, though this love is not for inanimate objects. It is the love of a vision to enable something better for those we impact. This lies at the core of user experience thinking.

Customer thinking or user thinking is really at the centre of any mission / purpose for most megaprojects and beyond. This purpose is all about creating a lifecycle for the asset and transforming it into one that exceeds expectations on lifestyle and quality of life for its users – all of which requires thinking through customer experience while designing and operating these huge components of a megaproject. When we design a megaproject, which is like a mini city, we have to make sure that we consider customer experience in the design process. We have to understand the guest experience aspect of facility management.

Many people think that FM is just a set of services provided to meet the demand of the users and make sure that the system is operating in a healthy way. However, the customer experience element is a cornerstone of facility management. We are there to ensure that we provide quality of life for users. This is an important aspect of any investment. In addition, we need to consider the importance of customer and end-user experience in the design of any development. This is a fundamental task while designing megaprojects. Planning customer experience includes components such as parking, easy access to buildings, sufficient wayfinding signage, etc. This has to be planned to the last point of detail, accounting for conditions for different seasons as an example, as well as the safety and comfort of the people using different facilities in these megaprojects. As a result, we need to analyse the design to ensure tools for enhancement of customer experience are seamlessly integrated.

It is important to move the thinking on customer experience from reactive methods to proactively seeking better integration while designing and operating a building. This becomes especially true in the case of megaprojects. Reactive customer experience is based on observing user needs and behaviour and adjusting offerings to suit trends that emerge. This remains a critical first step to set the context of how users engage with the built environment. However, the learning loop demands that we proactively seek better integration while designing and operating buildings. As already acknowledged, there is no such thing as a perfect design. We need to consider customer / end-user requirements in the design, and adjust the customer service offering within the facility during operation, especially in the first year.

Think about an existing megaproject you developed. Are you happy with the integration and lifestyle offering within this facility? Are your customer and end-user experiences exemplary? Does infrastructure such as roads, landscape, parking capacity and design of common areas, and amenities, contribute to creating a positive environment? These are all aspects to consider while planning the customer experience.

For example, when you have food retail in a building located close to parking areas, you will invariably end up with food odour issues in the parking lot. In new megaprojects or giga project developments, which are mixed-use, such facilities will have to be accounted for. Thus, it is important to design the development in such a way that operating certain units like restaurants will not impact the experience for other users like residents going to their apartments in the same tower. This then is an important element of continually improving the customer experience. I have seen many of these issues and mistakes repeated time and again. Do you need to walk for five to ten minutes to reach your car in humid weather in the summer in a multistorey car parking? This is a simple example of poor design.

Starting with accounting for operational parameters at the design stage, we need to consider the comfort and quality of life for different user types in a mixed-use development such as a megaproject. These user profiles extend across visitors going to restaurants and retail areas, occupants of the residential component, or officegoers with their workplaces in the same development.

However, these are the obvious user categories. We also need to consider the development users beyond these. Service providers who maintain the facilities are also its users and it is important to ensure that their experience is also enhanced. Doing this has a direct impact on their ability to efficiently deliver FM services at the development.

END-USER PAIN POINTS

As mentioned at the start of this chapter, getting feedback from users to identify their pain points and creating a culture of continuous improvement based on this is an important element for us FM practitioners to improve the environment and user experience. There are other ways of achieving this as well – by being more proactive in our approach through simulating the customer experience journey during the design process. By doing so, we can understand a user's pain while using the large communities within the megaprojects. Moreover, validating the different needs of end-users and guests during operation is critical to adjust design and services accordingly.

Once a megaproject has been made ready for operation, we need to take further steps to validate end-user and guest needs post-occupation. This is important for our success and to create more sustainable communities. Also, as FM subject matter experts, we have the experience from an operational background to create such synergies and make sure that we highlight all the pain points at the design stage. This will help us capture learnings and adjust designs of future megaprojects while enhancing the user experience in existing megaprojects.

OPERATOR BLIND SPOTS

The second aspect we consider in this chapter is operation / operators' blind spots – a very important factor to review. Normally, we, as operators of megaprojects, miss major opportunities for improvement. We don't look at the experience. We look at just the provision of services rather than linking service delivery, a key performance indicator, to customer experience.

This is a critical element of continuous improvement and fit for purpose within the facility. For FM companies taking over from the project, the task is not just to assume charge and provide service, but to also look at the experience of users in the first couple of years and link key performance indicators to customer experience. This will increase the satisfaction and quality of service that we provide to end-users and the needs of different users. This is a fundamental requirement to elevate and make any mega or giga project fit for purpose. Take, for instance, building a swimming pool – it is vital when building swimming pools in multi-storey facilities to create the right ambient environment for the pool to operate safely. We've all heard scary stories of kids getting injured or even losing their lives in these swimming pools if there aren't house rules like having parents around or employing lifeguards. But there are answers to minimising this possibility in design too. We can design swimming pools to ensure the right requirement, height, quality of water etc., so it is optimised and can be used by different users of the facilities, including children. This is just one example of how we can make sure that we don't just focus on providing the service, but also on the quality of life of users by enhancing safety measures, making sure that people are looked after and ensuring that we provide the services needed by users of these facilities.

Another pain point I have often observed in user experience is elevators and elevator management systems. If the wait time for an elevator during peak hours is more than ten minutes, we should look at ways to reduce this delay that is affecting the satisfaction of the user. We need to look at patterns of traffic that impact the use of these elevators and how can we use a smart artificial intelligence system within the elevator management system to optimise its efficiency, while also looking at schedules of different users and ways to manage spikes in elevator use by changing certain timings and activities.

In several contexts, we also need to account for privacy. Having visitors in a community without monitoring their entrances and exits and how they are accessing such a private amenity can be a major security risk. Another example is the need to make sure that the fire life safety of high-rise buildings is operational and integrated. We further need to ensure that the users and residents of the building are aware of these procedures. Normally everyone in the residences and office park retail knows their roles. It is everybody's responsibility when it comes to safety to protect themselves, their loved ones and others. This is one clear example where the FM operator of megaprojects with can have KPIs linked to customer experience.

VISIBILITY IS SYNERGY

Synergy is a clear outcome if we look at customer experience carefully and make a commitment to continuously improve the quality of life and, of course, enhance the satisfaction of the users and visitors of these megaprojects. This is an important pillar for FM service delivery since this will create synergy with the core business and will be a growth enabler. More visibility guarantees a quicker feedback loop and continuous improvement to meet the needs of different stakeholders – a clear sign of synergy.

As a result, for any megaproject to be a successful destination, we need to make sure that we have one hundred per cent clarity on the customers and their needs. We need to strike the balance between focus on providing services and customer experience as a driver for our success in megaprojects. The feedback loop is also intrinsic in improving how we operate these huge components of FM key result areas. This will help us create a better culture and allow us to have sustainability embedded within the users of such facilities. In doing so, we can create more synergy, make the environment better for everybody and help achieve our goals of establishing a sustainable long-term megaproject that works well for all stakeholders.

When customer experience becomes a critical success factor embedded in the FM development of a megaproject, it enables FM strategy to be linked deeper to the purpose of the core business of the organisation. In this way, customer experience is an important element of the FM strategy that will enable or have a bigger impact on these developments and their objectives, making a megaproject really shine.

Observe your facility operation at peak hours. Watch customer experience while using different parts of the facility. If you do what it takes to observe and catch trends, you can develop a proactive strategy. This will be the next pillar I cover, in addition to exploring the criticality of data in arriving at these conclusions.

As such, it's important for all of us involved in a project handover to not only look at the requirement of the facility but adjust these strategies based on the customer experience that we want to achieve and how we can increase the satisfaction level of these users of the facility.

In essence, this chapter covers the very important aspect of end-user pain points and how to address them. We have also looked at the blind spots for operators of these facilities and how visibility creates synergies to help us continuously improve efficiency, and environmental and social sustainability. Addressing this will make any giga or megaproject a destination that people would love to visit and experience.

CHAPTER 9

PILLAR 5: PROACTIVE STRATEGY AND DATA CRITICALITY

Consider Data-Centricity and Continuous Improvement as Key Drivers of Your Strategy

There was a time – not too long ago – that all of our travel was guided by paper maps and frequent course corrections as we got lost and had to double back. I grew up in the desert and the lack of features meant that we had to learn life hacks like navigating by the stars. It all seems so long ago but the reality is that widespread adoption of consumer navigation technologies is a trend no more than fifteen to twenty years old.

There is a sense of romance in the old navigation system of paper maps and course corrections. It all works very well and adds to the adventure of a holiday when one is on leisurely personal travel. But in critical situations or travel for urgent business work, for example, this old system was quite a liability. Modern GPS-based consumer navigation apps offer the advantage of data-driven insights for tasks as mundane as everyday commute. Imagine then, their impact on the management of large facilities and megaprojects, where there is little scope for trial and error. Where the concept of losing your way in operational delivery and circling back to course correct could result in a catastrophic impact on system efficiency, total cost of ownership or, worst of all, human safety and life.

I really like the way these modern customer navigation apps work. They are a stellar example of using customer-generated and crowdsourced data. These apps are able to predict estimated time of arrival at your destination by using deep analytics and rule applications with predictive trends based on traffic information and other conditions. It isn't a very complex science, just the contextual application of data generated by modern systems like GPS tracking, public information sources and data analytics sciences. Even better – with such real-time data, the system is able to constantly adjust to changing conditions and keep you informed of changing time estimates and advise on alternatives to address roadblocks that lie ahead.

It is the same with modern megaprojects. New-age equipment is a treasure trove of data that can enable proactive strategy based on predictive trends. This data is being generated and can be integrated and captured on a real-time or near real-time basis. The trick is to apply the right data sciences, system framework and insight delivery mechanisms to derive predictive insights.

THE IMPORTANCE OF INFORMATION IN MEGAPROJECTS AND HOW TO BEST HARNESS IT

Information is a great source of learning, but unless it is organised, processed, and made available to the right people in a format that enables decision-making, it becomes a burden, not a benefit. Continuous improvement is all about improving the result and at the core of this is converting data to information that will help better decision-making. Through this chapter, you will be able to understand the importance of collecting critical data to improve results and reduce costs where applicable. You will be able to go back to your work environment with a proactive approach to using data in the right context. You will be able to execute programs for continuous improvement, capturing details that will help you become a data-centric organisation when it comes to FM strategy formulation. It will also help you ensure input tasks are based on collecting data that help achieve expected outcomes.

Think about all existing megaprojects that you are managing. Do you collect and analyse data that enable closing gaps and improving reliability? This is a fundamental question that we need to ask ourselves since data helps us see if we are performing optimally or underperforming. So, we need to continually collect data and analyse it. This enables us to take calculated risks and is, therefore, an important initiative throughout the lifecycle of any megaproject.

There is an exercise called the post-optimisation program, where you make sure that you analyse data within the organisation that is providing FM services to the megaproject. The purpose of this exercise is to improve response time, reduce waste and increase efficiency. A great example is store and inventory management. It is wise to have critical and frequently used stock items available at all times, while ensuring that stock of slow-moving items do not put pressure on inventory space. Further, this can enable innovations such as moving to a model where the store for operations is a mobile store rather than one far away from the operation. By doing so, you can reduce the time wasted by technicians in going back and forth to stores, thereby increasing their efficiency and improving response times to result in a better customer experience. This is a simple example of looking at your inventory strategy, where you can implement a preventive maintenance routine by reducing the handoff, having needed spares and consumables available as well as looking at your transportation strategy. These also play an important role in cost optimisation programs as you look to take the right decisions through insights from collected data.

Data about time spent in travel, technician time in executing preventive maintenance, or getting spares are among other data points that you collect throughout the whole process of achieving or accomplishing your work orders. It is important to collect data – not just about activities, but also related to customer requirements, service levels targeted and, importantly, operational parameters for the different systems within buildings.

QUICK WINS AND WASTE REDUCTION

Having a plan and strategy based on data will enable you to become proactive in your approach. For example, if you collect data from customer feedback on the comfort of the user, you can easily adjust the operational requirements of end use.

Going forward in this chapter, we define the first important success element as having a proactive strategy and related data that will help gain from quick wins and reduced waste. Of course, this will be the result of optimising the use of data-based action. Megaprojects can focus quick wins on service, quality improvement and effectiveness. This is an important aspect to be considered, especially for critical services where we need to provide services such as avoiding interruption of power, and sustained availability of water and air-conditioning. Continuous operation of critical and basic services, especially during peak hours, is critical. Accordingly, we need to develop a method to achieve quick wins and reduce waste by collecting data that helps optimise operator actions.

As you look at diagnosing issues and pain points with the involvement of the right FM consultant as a doctor, implement the project birth certificate approach in the development and then move to customer experience (all aspects covered in previous chapters), you will realise the value of data collected to help get quick wins and reduce waste.

ENGAGING TOOLS TO INCREASE COMPETENCIES

The second important point of this chapter is about engaging tools to increase competencies, and this is an obvious benefit of proactive strategy and data criticality. This will help us involve stakeholders in the continuous improvement exercise and ensure skills are developed to achieve expected outcomes. Continuous improvement and fit for purpose facility approach is the result and once we have the right strategy with data at its the centre, we can engage the different stakeholders. This will also help us improve resource efficiencies, reduce waste and, eventually, improve the lifecycle performance of megaprojects.

BETTER INTEGRATION

The third point is about better integration. I spoke earlier about how one aspect of FM is about reflex / muscle memory and the instinct that it enables. However, available data resources can ensure that this is augmented by insights based on actual performance, enhancing the contextual understanding of a situation before deciding on a course of action. Again, when we have data, we can take proactive action to create integration. The criticality of collecting and analysing data is that it helps improve integration and reduce communication gaps and waste. This is an important element to help avoid making blind ad-hoc decisions. Also, when you make a decision without having data, it is always going to create a communication gap between the different stakeholders and result in waste of effort and resources. This can be avoided if we have data as a central focus of our operation.

A simple example of having critical data-based improvements is when you look at electrical short circuits in different zones of the building and analyse why this may be happening. Is it user breach and behaviour, or poor maintenance in these areas that is causing a short circuit? When you collect data, the most important exercise is analysing it to help you reach the right conclusion that allows you to put a revised plan into action.

Data is the core of Impactful FM strategy in megaprojects. Data analysis and related lessons learnt are critical success factors for FM delivery enhancement at any mega or giga project. This will enable the implementation of a more effective FM strategy that will result in enhanced building life and help manage user expectations. In this strategy to collect data while performing different services, sometimes simple tools like computer-aided FM (CAFM) systems prove to be a rich source of quality assurance on data collection. These help us to look at the effectiveness and efficiency of operation on a weekly or even daily basis. Having a building management system (BMS) where we bring together information about the different predictive alarms for various systems and energy consumption helps assess if we are managing our building in the right way with energy efficiency being the result while outages are minimised.

DATA-DRIVEN DECISION MAKING

As I mentioned, data-driven decision-making during operations is a critical success factor for any FM strategy. Do keep in mind the benefits of applying data-driven decision-making approaches and their amplification in the context of mega and giga projects, where they can be force-multipliers. These benefits include enhanced ease of achieving financial savings and sustainability objectives. Such data-driven decision-making also facilitates superior customer experience. Looking dynamically and proactively at our strategy to harness collected data can help us further in achieving our objective and become a sustainable megaproject in the short, medium and long term.

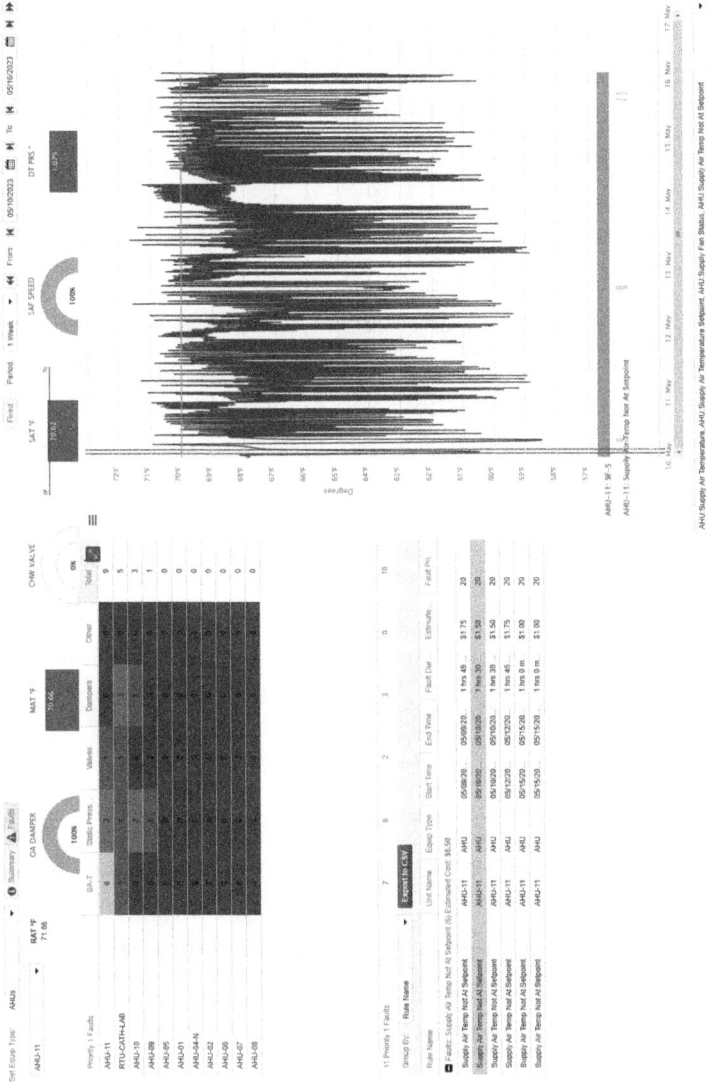

The dashboard that you see above is a detailed analysis of an individual HVAC system. It provides intelligent analysis and not just a parameter view of equipment operations data. It is a flexible and interactive dashboard that allows analysis of issues. Technology here helps facility operators to efficiently analyse reliable data without having to switch between screens or needing any coding knowledge.

For instance, if we observe facility operation at peak hours and analyse the data source, we can use this data to improve effectiveness and customer satisfaction. When the facility is operating at its peak (i.e., when the maximum number of users are present in the building) and the weather condition is harsh, you can understand the operational parameters of the system at full capacity of various facilities. This is where you can analyse data from the system that will help you identify patterns to further improve your approach to managing, operating and maintaining this building. This is the joy of collecting data, analysing it and finally making a decision that is based on facts that enhance your own expertise and adeptness and reading trends to make decisions.

Data abounds for diverse aspects of FM operations like health and safety parameters and hygiene, for example. We can correlate data about weather conditions (often from accurate public sources) with customer indications of need and their feedback on the various systems to set parameters that can trigger pre-alarms based on algorithms.

We can enhance the health of systems while also looking at energy consumption with comparisons of day-to-day, month-to-month and year-to-year trends. There are innumerable examples of how having data that is actionable results in proactive decision-making. These examples also act as indications of how a data-driven strategy is a critical component of FM having the right impact on megaprojects.

CASE IN POINT: DUBAI SILICON OASIS

In the context of data structuring, I'd like to come back to my favourite example of a thriving megaproject: Dubai Silicon Oasis. This development has always insisted on incorporating a proactive data-driven strategy. The FM team has been encouraged to collect information about all the various users, systems, and weather conditions and bring them all together to formulate the right equation to make the right decision, thereby improving culture and eventually saving on costs to help the megaproject to be more sustainable. This approach has also helped keep all stakeholders satisfied and end-users enjoying quality of life while using this facility. Dubai Silicon Oasis is a large mixed-use community of residential, retail, schools and hospitals, offices, malls, and hotels – data from all these assets is collected in a central location so it can be cross-referenced to establish the right proactive strategy and have a higher impact on the whole development.

THE ESSENCE

We have highlighted in this chapter how data is a critical component of FM operations and how, if we collect data diligently and in the right structure, we can create the right equation to ensure our success in megaprojects and make a strong impact on its sustainability, and financial and social components. These methods help us communicate with the different stakeholders, engaging them in our proactive strategy and gaining more data to help us manage stakeholder satisfaction and improve operation, team competency and building maintenance standards. This seamlessly ties in with the next pillar, which emphasises how data can be used as an invaluable tool for those who operate in a pilot position at a megaproject.

CHAPTER 10

PILLAR 6: PILOT POSITION

Technology-Driven FM Strategy for
Giga and Megaprojects

I do not fear computers. I fear the lack of them. Everybody gets so much information all day long that they lose their common sense. Technology will help us in a big way to convert big data into useful information that enables effective action to be taken accordingly.

My visit to the city of St. Louis, Missouri was an eye-opener in this regard. I have covered the details of the technology-driven operations style adopted by the city in earlier chapters. But seeing a central point for data coming in from over 3,300 buildings and all of this data being analysed for impactful decision-making made me see the true definition of the "control" in "control room".

When I say "pilot" position, I mean that metaphor literally. Having well-organised data will enable you to have full clarity – much like a pilot flying an aircraft. I have highlighted this analogy in detail earlier when talking about the pilot room concept and will reiterate it here: when you see all the data that is generated while operating mega and giga projects, you realise the depth of information coming in from various infrastructure elements, building services systems, power meters, pre-alarms, financial utilities spend per system / zone / day / hour / month and kilowatt consumption. Public sources also allow easy access to daily and hourly weather conditions, and weather forecast information. We also have the ability to capture a lot of information that filters in through different systems, such as the CAFM software on spare parts, replacements, preventive work orders, corrective and reactive and emergency work orders, guest profiles and so on.

This is what prompts the need for technology. We must use technology to our advantage – not just to capture work orders but to seamlessly integrate with the Industry 4.0 revolution driven by the internet of things (IoT), smart sensing and autonomous systems. Technology should be embedded within operations in a way that helps extract data and convert it to information that will help us assume the pilot position in a megaproject.

At its core, the definition of a megaproject is its size – it is huge and complex with critical systems located underground, above the ground, or on the roof of an existing structure. Each of these systems is very important for the safety of users and the reliability of such systems enables success in megaprojects. So, if we want to make sure that people are safe and comfortable with a high quality of life, and we are also looking at the sustainability element, we need to create this pilot position. Without technology backing our own FM subject matter expertise, we will not be able to do so.

This is the transition that we need to consider while creating a proactive strategy for any megaproject. We understand that data is critical. We understand that customer experience is important as we covered in the previous chapters. We understand that the handover and the planning phases are important. Given all of this, the aim is to be in a pilot position for these big projects where we can make the right decisions and operate in the right way. Ultimately, by end of this chapter, we should be able to understand that collecting important critical data is not easy without having technology tools to help us, especially in megaprojects.

VISIBILITY ACROSS ALL ASPECTS

This is where we need to understand that it is crucial for all of us to set a robust technology strategy, one that allows us to have more visibility of all aspects of facility operations. It is also important for us to adopt this pilot position using technology, so we can empower our teams to enhance system performance and resource competency, which are the fundamental objectives of using technology. We should also establish realistic KPIs, such that we can easily understand facility health conditions in their context. We have a lot of information that tells us about the facility's condition. However, if we are not bringing these data points together in an organised manner, it will not reach the right people to inform them about the health of the condition of the facility. It is important for us to move to the next level by creating a pilot position using technology and subject matter expertise as facility managers, to ensure that we bring information and put it in the right context for us to take the right decisions. Think about it – in all existing megaprojects you are managing, using technology effectively to collect information about resources, completion rate and competency, system performance, customer experience and facility energy and sustainability behaviour can be a clever way to enable smart living.

I started my journey looking for technology that will help us integrate and gather information from the various systems and the various platforms that we use to operate our buildings – be it a building management system, CAFM, or specialist systems for elevator management, weather condition monitoring, and utility builds, amongst others. I have increasingly focused on identifying smarter ways to integrate all information from these systems into one platform, which then creates the opportunity to build data lakes from which nuggets of data can be drawn and analysed to present the right actionable information.

BUILDING TOTAL CONSUMPTION TREND

COST REDUCTION COMPARISON 2021 vs 2019

COOLING ENERGY

COST REDUCTION COMPARISON 2021 vs 2020

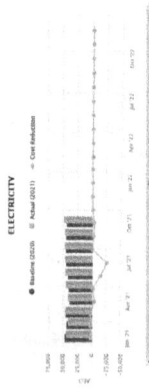

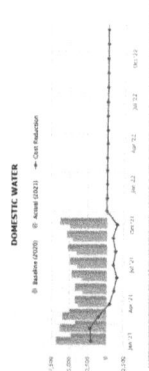

COOLING ENERGY

DOMESTIC WATER

DOMESTIC WATER

ELECTRICITY

ELECTRICITY

This is a great example of how FM managers and building owners can be presented with a combination of analysed and raw real-time data from across input systems. With actionable baselines for them to visually identify deviations and points of concern, they can view data in a single glance view.

KNOW THE PROBLEM (WHERE AND HOW)

In my ambition to identify the right source systems and analytical methods, the intent has always been to provide enough visibility into diverse parameters for all internal stakeholders. To enable this, it becomes important to integrate the diverse systems across a megaproject – this is the primary enabler of a pilot's position (and of the pilot room concept) that helps manage megaprojects. Often megaprojects, such as developments comprising ports and free zones cover more than a hundred kilometres of roads and buildings and port operations. Such mega projects are increasingly becoming strong sources of economic growth across the Middle East region and, in such large operations, pilot positions are critical to ensure smooth and efficient operations.

In the example I have highlighted about St. Louis, I have seen in action how all information is brought into a large, centralised data lake, ready to be analysed by FM experts. The first step in this, and the main point of this chapter, is the FM expert coordination with technology providers to ensure that the technology platform reflects a deep understanding of real problems and solution areas that technology can help support on.

Without technology bringing information and correlating data from different systems, we will not know the problem. For example, if there is a call out on a system that was maintained recently, a quick method is required to run a root cause analysis to identify whether the problem lies with the maintenance procedure, the competency of the technician or whether some factor caused this failure. In this context, well-structured technology tools will help identify aspects from when the operator last visited the asset for maintenance. During this inspection, did they notice an unusual noise? Did they get any other indication that pointed to potential failure? Did they follow the standard operating procedure (SOP) for preventive maintenance correctly, or have they done it in a way that actually created the problem?

With a single source of data, new data coming in helps analyse the root cause of a problem to tell us more about what had happened over the last month, what is happening right now and what had happened a few hours before the call-out. Such comparison-based performance analysis is a great way to validate the gaps and performance issues while operating a large-scale facility. This cannot happen easily without technology, and we can end up floundering as we seek solutions to ensure that these types of incidents do not recur.

ANALYSIS WITH CLARITY

The other benefit of establishing a pilot position is clarity and deep analysis. When you have a customer complaining about an air conditioning system, you can always analyse with clarity, based on factors such as when the maintenance was done, how old the system is, what the weather condition is and influencing factors such as humidity leakage and whether the external door was open for longer than usual. Ultimately, this enables analysis with clarity on the behaviour of the building during various periods – for example, the same time yesterday and even last month. This is why we have an advantage by creating a pilot position strategy, where we all information has been brought to one place.

Another example is when we have a failure of any system. If we have data on pre-alarms, maintenance and performance history of the equipment in a single data repository, we can proactively anticipate if there is a need to upgrade, replace or enhance the system to avoid disturbance to our operation and the quality of life of the building.

INCREASED RELIABILITY

I still remember from early in my career, a flooding that took place in one of the most critical basement buildings for telecom operations. This caused outage in telecom service to customers. Incidents of this nature, if not rectified early, can have an impact on customer confidence, brand value, operating costs, and cost of equipment replacement – all of it eventually impacting business viability. In this instance, we realised that the source of flooding was water leaking from a huge fountain pump room located on the same floor. If we had water sensors and operations status of this water fountain circulation system, we could have avoided this major risk of losing connectivity in telecom systems providing services to a significant portion of that particular city.

By creating a pilot position, the focus moves to using various pieces of information that are brought from different systems. This helps establish a pilot platform that will enable technology-based proactive operations. For example, if you get information about the energy efficiency of a central cooling system while looking at maintenance and breakdown history, you will find the factors that contribute to the problem and long-term impact on cost, customer satisfaction and environmental criteria. This will be clear as all information is brought to one central location.

This is the ultimate goal of having the technology to enable FM to be more proactive in achieving its goal of enhancing the quality of life of users and FM operations. For example, you can always use technology to monitor freezers in a store or supermarket. You don't need to wait until the refrigerator fails. With an IoT-enabled sensor connected through the internet and a dashboard provided on the mobile of the store's operation duty manager, it is possible to monitor if the temperature in these freezers has increased by more than two degrees. This means either the freezer is not cooling, or the door is open. By taking proactive, corrective action, food spoilage can be avoided. This is where technology can help us act and be proactive in our operations, thus becoming the pilot we want to be, to prevent further losses and improve operations.

Imagine if all megaprojects embedded necessary technology-based systems and strategy during design. Sustainability would be achieved from the get-go and we would have a bigger impact on FM and the megaproject.

As you can see from our discussion in this chapter, a technology-based operation is not an option anymore. To become sustainable, you will need to create a pilot room, which is critical to driving the effectiveness of total cost of ownership. This is why we have allocated a full chapter to talk about creating the pilot room. We need to start looking at the facility operation mode and how we can digitise operations to collect more data and integrate people, buildings and technology while automating processes.

This will certainly help the operation team, rather than policing them. We will have more insight into the challenges of performing preventive maintenance and why these activities may be taking more time than standard. Further, we can learn why they took more time to attend to a failure and why this emergency happened in the first place. Is there something we can do to avoid repeated callouts, considering that a lot of such callouts are repeats – occurring day after day, month after month, or year after year without anybody tackling the root cause?

By using technology, we can evaluate the competency of people, their training needs, and the availability of spares and tools. We can understand more about the pain of the building and its customer and users. Another very important aspect is the health and safety of building users – we can co-opt building users into the facility management process to ensure that safety becomes everybody's responsibility.

The ultimate goal is to protect everybody and having smarter buildings will help in this endeavour. We need to automate our processes to help collect more data using technology and achieve our goal of optimising and creating further synergy. This is why we need to have the right FM strategy in place from as early as design and do commissioning and testing activities in the building to create the project birth certificate at this stage. As a result, we can collect more information about the pain of the users and the customer experience, and gather data to generate insights based on the power of collective information.

Technology integrates and organises data for us, and helps us see how relevant different information is, how we can organise this information to assess the various problems and challenges, and analyse with clarity to improve reliability.

Creating the pilot position for a megaproject is not an easy task and it could take one to three years to achieve. In fact, I would say that it typically takes three years to have a fully-fledged pilot room that helps us make the right decisions and operate a megaproject with health of assets as a core focus area.

Now that we see how important it is to be looking at occupying the pilot position in megaprojects, the next step is to scale up to get further benefits.

CHAPTER 11

PILLAR 7: SCALE UP FOR IMPACT

Nuclear Impact Is Enabled by Sharing Data across Similar-Use Buildings

An FM professional is a multi-faceted personality. If I have been successful in communicating my intent through various examples I have provided in previous chapters, you will understand that we FM professionals bring to our craft the insight of an analyst, the logic of an engineer, the instinct of a seasoned professional, the observation skills of a sociologist and anthropologist, and the introspective mindset of a philosopher. Let me add another skill requirement for FM professionals here: the analytical prowess of an economist.

Seeing trends in multitudes of data is a key capability that the new-age, multi-tasking FM practitioner has to include in their professional skill repertoire. In the age of technology-enabled decisions by data, degree of accuracy is a direct outcome of the quality of insights, which itself is a result of the quantum of data points – more data points imply more accurate quality of insights that can be drawn from them. This is what eventually adds to the ability to create an Impactful FM culture in megaprojects and beyond.

In the previous chapter, we covered the pilot position concept as an important one in megaprojects, focused on bringing information of different systems into a central location, integrated in such a manner that you can do effective data analysis.

Now, we'll talk about not just bringing data from different systems, but also bringing data from different buildings that have similar use and behaviour. This enables a scale-up model, based on data that can be compared. For example, the education sector can witness true transformation by having data from a hundred schools pouring into one data lake from across different systems. A big data lake can be very powerful for anybody who is managing megaprojects. It is important to scale up so we can ultimately get nuclear impact and realise the synergy that we can get by connecting hundreds of buildings that have similar use within one or more megaprojects and bringing all this information to one big data lake.

Large number of megaprojects of similar use, such as schools, hospitals, government buildings, airports, and malls, among other mixed-use mega and giga projects, getting connected to one central data warehouse creates the opportunity to conduct effective benchmarking. Based on these benchmarks, FM expertise can be centralised using technology to convert information into a useful, actionable plan.

In a megaproject, the pilot is not just for one aeroplane. Conceptually in this case, it is one pilot flying several aeroplanes at once. A central control room where you can see all infrastructure systems and assets across different buildings and different mixed-use developments acts as the nerve centre for megaprojects. The massive amounts of data brought into one place, from systems across maintenance, weather conditions, utility consumption trends and bills from different buildings within the megaproject can help create source to draw benchmark trends and create feedback loops to address variance in performance of operators of different buildings. Ultimately, you can get better recommendations and outcomes once you have this data converted to an actionable plan.

By the end of this chapter, you will see how FM impact can be unlimited once you gather more critical data from the various facilities within different megaprojects. Gap analysis and improvement opportunities are innumerable, if data collation is done right, and in a structured manner. Once you scale up your connectivity, you can create a data lake to reflect on the learning to improve future facility design. It's not just about improving efficiencies in existing megaprojects, but also continuous improvement in the design of similar megaprojects in the future.

Also, by the end of this chapter, you will definitively see how to make scale-up more effective, with different expertise and data scientists working together. We have to rely not just on expertise from subject matter experts, but also on data scientists because coordinating and organising data requires people who are specialised in managing it. There is the cliché that states "knowledge is power". If this is true, then what are we waiting for? Let us scale up and improve through gathering information. This will help us set up the required operational strategies based on buildings' demands, systems' conditions, weather conditions and user profiles. The outcomes are proven. In the St. Louis case study, I have highlighted in earlier chapters, such interconnectivity across the 3300+ buildings has resulted in a rapid reduction of operational and energy costs by 20%. Imagine the sheer quantum of saving this 20% translates into over something as large as an urban agglomeration.

POSITIVE MAGNITUDE IMPACT

Data is power but human intellect is the real transformative agent. You can implement all kinds of technology but ultimately, the success of such systems is the result of human FM subject matter expertise in technology stack design and implementation. We will now delve deeper into the positive impact of technology combined with human expertise. To know what is truly going on through data, you can create transformation through scaling up and bringing more data from different facilities into one data lake. There is a positive impact because you will know what is happening in the different facilities. Once you get comparable system data, you can easily list the variables and issues when it comes to operational challenges, team skills and quality outcomes. Of course, the quality of the building design and user behaviour can improve the outcome by looking at the change in input. A gap analysis will be more effective once increasing amounts of data is collected from similar-use buildings.

This is clear in the example of St. Louis, and we need to advise the developer of a megaproject to have a strong connectivity strategy for all their buildings and systems channelled into one place. From there, we can create a data lake and get data scientists to work closely with the FM experts to guide operators and users of these buildings and infrastructure to place optimisation and sustainability at the top of the agenda. We can realise positive impact through this process by being aware of what is going on, rather than having a resident engineer in all these developments. This results in significant saving – not just on energy and running costs, but also in operating facilities.

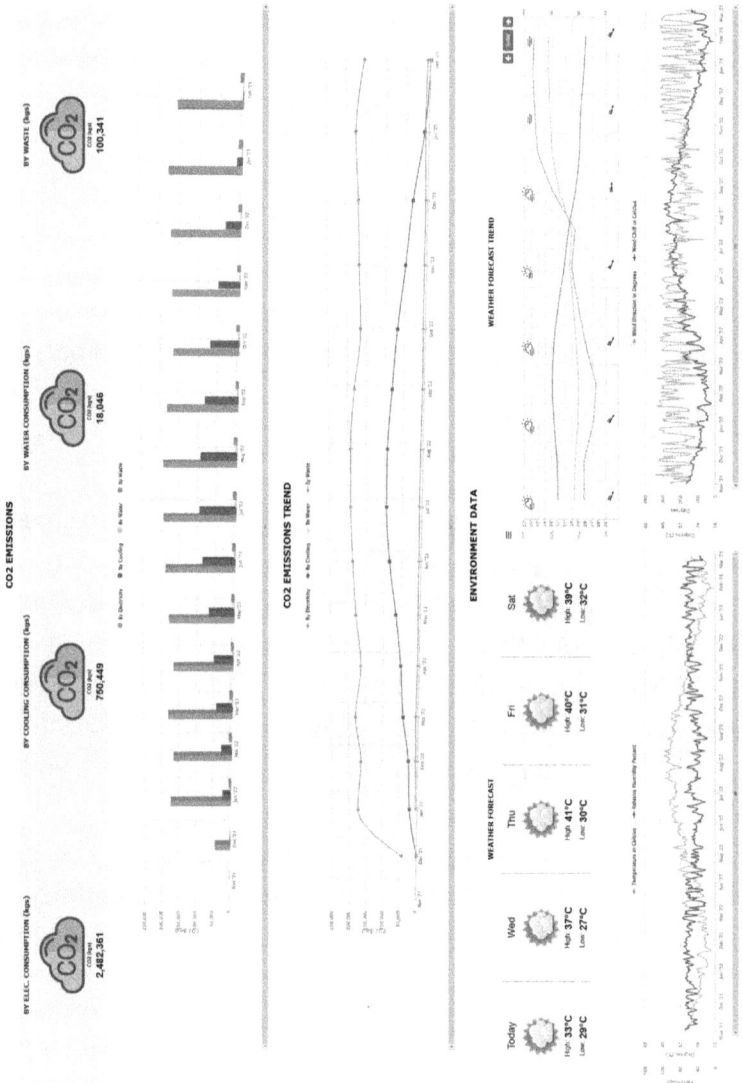

The above is an example of how data comes together from different sources to enable developments to be more sustainable.

SCALE UP THE IMPACT

In addition to scaling up data connectivity, it becomes important to also scale up the impact and verification process – the second point on this subject. This is a continuation of the first point, which is knowing what's going on. The more data you have from the different buildings (ideal from one hundred similar use buildings and more), the more effective the analysis is. This also provides a wider dataset for verification. Of course, cross-functional resources can be used rather than placing resources in a geographical area. In this way, people can troubleshoot while sitting in the command control and recommendation reports can be issued based on the data available and coordination between site operation teams and the central team. Scale-up will help us verify and have a real-time impact, continuous improvement to overcome design and operational challenges and often help address user challenges as well.

It's pertinent that we conceptualise the scale-up strategy, analyse what is going on and how we can scale up the connectivity to get strong benefits across all facilities. We can then measure and verify these outcomes.

One great example is FM operations for supertall buildings. It is important to ensure that such facilities have a pilot position where all elements of the supertall building can be connected to ensure effective analysis, because several components of supertall buildings operate in areas that are hard to access or monitor regularly. In this case, it is important to not just have the right pilot room set up, but the right pilot, i.e., the right subject matter expert to analyse the data that is streaming in from the many different areas and on the various parameters that drive FM operations. This person should be able to analyse the data from various systems and implement pre-alarm measures that will help avoid shutdown and breakdown and have a continuous improvement plan.

TRUE SMART CITY APPROACH

The city is the ultimate manifestation of a giga project. By scaling up and getting more data into one big data lake, we will end up with more critical and non-critical use buildings connected within the city. For example, in a city with many megaprojects, if all elevator system data is gathered and connected, a lifecycle assessment can be easily conducted as to which elevators are safe and more effective, looking at the different factors that might have an impact on their performance. Ultimately, this is another way of showcasing sustainability as a reflection of a smart city. This is where the scale-up helps organise data, talk to vendors and suppliers of different systems to improve design, improve skills of people who are operating and maintaining the systems, and make sure that future designs are more effective and intelligent. That is the ultimate goal when we scale up.

If all megaprojects contribute to scale-up data collection for their operation and energy, the impact will be phenomenal. The takeaway from this chapter is once you scale up and bring data of various similar-use buildings together, you will be surprised by the power of such information. Ultimately, FM subject matter experts will give the right strategy and advice that will help the FM team to operate the building effectively, thereby achieving optimal quality of life for building users. This will also enable FM companies and teams to help the core business of the facility to achieve its objectives.

It's always good to have data, but it's also good to make this data relevant and get the right team in a centralised place where they can see data on various projects, buildings and developments, not just in one country, but across the world. Developing such important benchmark information will help us become more effective in operating and maintaining and, of course, designing future projects, thereby improving the total cost of ownership.

Also, we need to start combining information data of all users in various similar-use buildings to ensure harmony and create the required benchmarks. I am sure a lot of people are asking for service level agreements, and these SLAs can be published as a guideline and sometimes even as design review basis from an FM perspective on a project. Ultimately, it is very difficult to make such a checklist unique or general. This is why if we have enough information about what's going on in the existing building, we can always have the right checklist and standards that can be categorised based on the use and objective of these facilities, since we already have vital information that tells us what to do and how we are actually doing today.

Consequently, it's important for all of us to look at buildings, not just people. As stated earlier in the chapter, this is ultimately the role of the doctor. Without the right tools (like those for scanning the heart and different body parts), the doctor cannot give the right recommendations and remedy. Similarly, by having a data lake and a data scientist at their side, the FM subject matter expert will be able to get the correct guidelines for future megaprojects to be built the right way, and to establish the required long-term strategy for existing megaprojects and beyond. This will also enable the right approach to controlling the total cost of ownership. We will be achieving essential development goals: ensuring the quality of life of the users and facilities are achieved and, most importantly, achieving our sustainability objective.

A clear example of the importance of creating benchmarks is different for industries like hospitality in say, the classification of five-star, four-star and three-star hotels. Similar methods can be adopted when it comes to schools and other facilities from an FM perspective. This involves looking at energy consumption, user satisfaction, the operational sustainability of the building and how the total cost of ownership impacts the overall building.

Again, we need to start combining all users' information and data of various similar-use buildings to make sense of similarities and differences. Ultimately, this will help us to set up the right service level agreement that the owners and users of the buildings expect from the team managing facilities and megaproject assets. The FM team can reflect on the right key performance indicators for the various service providers on the supply side that can match the demand of end-users and the owner of the facility.

Megaprojects are challenging because we have a lot of scattered data and aren't always able to bring this data together and make it relevant to the FM organisation and the owner – where they can execute sustainable data-driven facility management. This will ultimately help us achieve our sustainability goal of influencing the total cost of ownership. Of course, integrating information is crucial; however, it is the use of technology tools – not just a human as a subject matter expert – and data scientists that will help us reach the next level.

This is what we will discuss in the next chapter when we talk about the disruptive technology-based FM strategy.

CHAPTER 12

PILLAR 8: DISRUPTIVE TECHNOLOGY IN FM

At the Heart of New-Era Impactful FM:
Directing Technological Disruption towards
Sustainable FM Strategies for Megaprojects

In previous chapters, I outlined the importance of data and of having the right analysis done to enable truly Impactful FM. I briefly touched upon the concept of technology that enables this data to be converted into powerful insights. This chapter is dedicated to the major innovation that is happening in the field of technology – across equipment, computing hardware and data analytics software – to drive this process.

With the large number of megaprojects of similar use, there are always opportunities for FM impact to be multiplied, considering technology as a core of the operation of closed or scattered similar projects such as schools, hospitals, government buildings, airports, malls, among other mixed-use mega and giga projects. Therefore, all of us need to digitise and use technology in our day-to-day FM operations. This is how FM impact can be multiplied to get to a nuclear pattern.

The impact of new-age techniques like artificial intelligence and machine learning (AI / ML) is being seen in the form of diverse use cases. ML algorithms such as building fault detection rules and training the machine to learn from initial stage human experiences can enable megaproject owners to achieve sustainability and convert FM into the core enabler of success. Ultimately, when you bring all information into an FM data lake facility, it's not just the data expertise and the data scientists who will help multiply the impact. Technology is also intrinsic in improving building operations.

So, what are the technology tools that we need to use? Of course, we need to use machine learning. We need to implement fault rule detection algorithms that will enable the right action without human interference to take the right action at the right time.

By end of this chapter and this book, you will be able to conclude that FM impact can be unlimited by using technology as a powerful tool to effectively manage the lifecycle of projects.

This is the transformation that we need to aim for. As a baseline, we need to have people and subject-matter experts, but without technology, we will witness information overload. Without using technology tools to help us predict failure and drop in performance, as well as learn more about the patterns, subject matter experts on equipment will not be able to analyse fast or effectively enough. For example, you need to use technology in FM as a powerful tool to manage risks related to HSE (and not just to control the lifecycle) while ensuring the core business organisation is growing within mega and giga projects.

Technology will allow us to effectively manage the lifecycle and risks in megaprojects and large parts of a city. In such large-scale developments, it is challenging to manage assets individually as there are financial and service skill limitations. Hence, FM experts must utilise design technology-based tools such as fault detection rules and machine learning. As the foundation of strategic initiatives, these need to be seamlessly connected with IoT sensors and FM operation automation where possible.

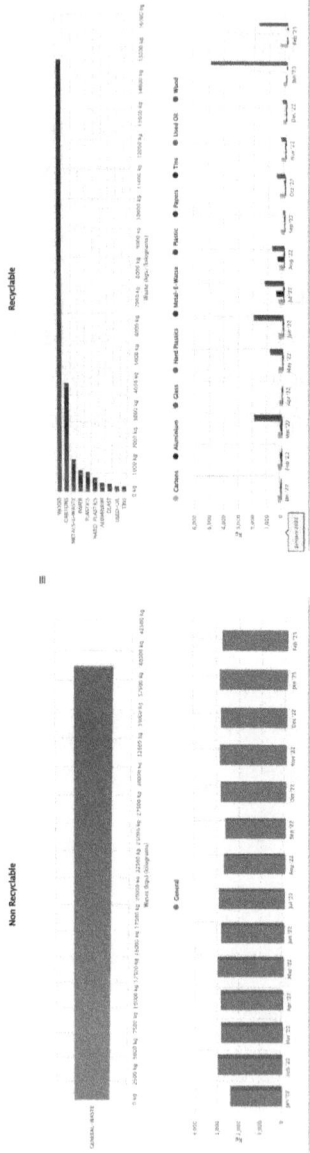

INSIGHTS INTO WASTE MANAGEMENT DATA COLLECTION AND IMPACT
ANALYSIS AT MEGAPROJECTS

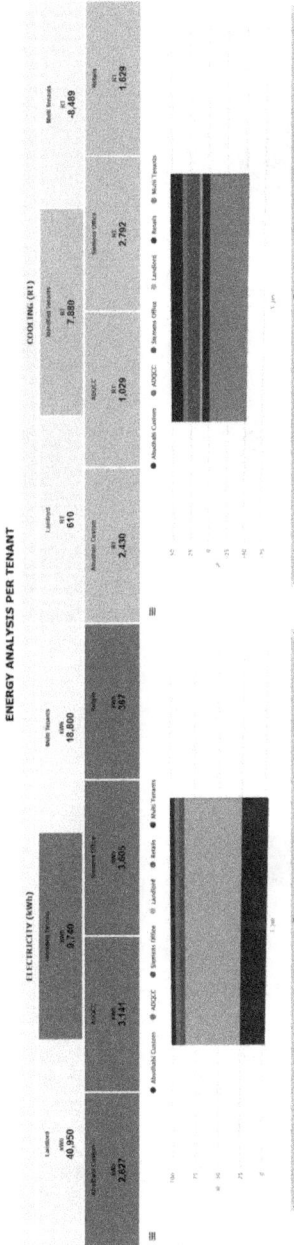

ENERGY ANALYSIS PER TENANT

FLOOR WISE ENERGY BREAKDOWN

SYSTEMS WISE ENERGY BREAKDOWNS (ELECTRICITY)

SUB METERS ELECTRIC CONSUMPTION RANKING

ACTIONABLE ANALYSIS OF ENERGY USING TECHNOLOGY-EMBEDDED TOOLS

THE LEADERS WHO DRIVE FM ARE WHAT MAKE IT IMPACTFUL

LEADERSHIP WITH PASSION

Leadership with passion is the first element of success for embracing technology in all three levels of FM operations: strategic, tactical and operational.

The key takeaway from this chapter is the importance of leadership and a focused FM approach to transforming operations in any megaproject and beyond. So, we can always talk about technology digitalisation and transformation, but without leadership, all such initiatives will have limitations. It is prudent that we use case studies to highlight the value of technology and disruptive tools to help subject matter experts and data scientists while acknowledging that passionate leaders will promote change.

Leadership as a culture needs to be embraced to ensure that the change process that comes with technology integration is managed effectively. For example, how can we assemble and encourage stakeholders to work together? We have different stakeholders – building owners, megaproject owners, investors and owner representatives as well as construction stakeholders (designer, main contractor, project manager and subcontractors). Aligning the interests of these stakeholders will require leadership in all aspects.

Moving onto the operation aspect, the important issue to address is bringing stakeholders like operation FM providers, operation teams, end-users and government entities to buy into this change process. All these stakeholders need to be engaged. Without leadership, true passion for the work and clear intent to achieve sustainability goals, we will have limitations in applying facility management. The practice of using technology at a megaproject level will provide incredible financial, social and environmental sustainability advantages. Without strong leadership, this is a challenge. We need to have leaders. We need to empower the team.

More than simply appointing leaders, we need to facilitate a leadership culture. We need to make people passionate about managing the total cost of ownership and make buildings, developments and cities at large more sustainable.

PASSION WITH DRIVE

Being passionate about what we do helps build a culture of leadership. But this is not enough. Once we become passionate leaders, we need to have a sense of drive at every stage. With a culture of passion and drive, FM impact on financial, sustainability, social and engagement aspects can be tremendous. We can achieve this by employing people who are resilient, agile and think out of the box. Engaging different subject matter experts to help us to achieve our aim is important, and this is what we are trying to do when we talk about passion with drive.

This is also what I have actually seen in action at projects like Silicon Oasis or St. Louis, where we had different stakeholders who are passionate leaders, driving results on a daily basis.

DRIVE WITH RESULT

When you drive a project, the ultimate goal is to get results while celebrating each step of the way to maintain a positive culture. We need to change traditional thinking and create one driven by an analytical approach. We need to set up the right technology rules to avoid overloading and overspending so we can achieve results. This is what we mean when we discuss the importance of pride with results. Being agile and resilient is critical in managing the variables and stakeholder influences.

We need to remember that winning is a habit, and success is a choice. And, looking at the different case studies, this was especially true during my involvement in Burj Khalifa. Here, we had leadership and we were passionate about the project because it was (and is) the tallest tower in the world. We had to drive results and create a data-driven culture. Technology has ultimately helped us achieve that. What if all megaprojects could have leadership with vision, passion with teamwork and spirit, and drive? The impact of FM strategy can be enormous, and this is an important driver of our success. We need to talk about leadership, strategic thinking and planning, how to bring people together and how to lead them on the path to success.

It is important to build a winning mentality and reward the team every step of the way, rather than waiting for the reward to be at the end of the project. If we all aim to achieve sustainability using an effective approach that engages people and technology and understands building challenges, design and user experience, we can apply this at the design, construction and operational stages, which will have a significant impact on the total cost of ownership and propel us into a new era of mega and giga projects. Leadership will be more resilient, and we can aim to become more sustainable. We need to have leadership and project management skills so we can become accountable and more transparent about the roles and responsibilities of every stakeholder.

This starts when we bring all useful information and data of similar-use projects together to result in a nuclear impact for all the leaders. As we have noted, machine learning, fault detection rules and data lake management are at the core of impactful FM operations. This happens once we have established a core data pilot position, engaged a proactive strategy based on data criticality, driven customer experience, and involved the doctor to find the right prevention rather than preparing a cure.

If a cure is needed, the doctor has the necessary medicine that will help us, but ultimately, we need the willingness of the patient and, of course, the various stakeholders. This is critical in understanding and diagnosing the problems.

Moreover, we must improve the customer experience, achieve the pilot project, make decisions informed by data criticality, and, ultimately, scale up and achieve a sustainable FM strategy based on disruptive technology. I would like to again acknowledge that leadership culture, drive, FM skills, and data and technology-based decision-making are key elements in your FM strategy success in megaprojects.

CONCLUSION

This book is intended to act as the cornerstone for the FM profession to drive the new era of sustainable development of existing and future cities. Following the path laid out in the eight pillars of Impactful FM will pave the way forward. By doing this, asset owners can be proud of their developments while implementing sustainability (environmental, social and governance) parameters.

FM BEST PRACTICE DRIVEN BY TECHNOLOGY WILL TAKE US ALL THE WAY TO CONTROL THE TOTAL COST OF OWNERSHIP WHILE IMPROVING USER EXPERIENCE AND CREATING A STRONG DEVELOPMENT BRAND. THE IMPLEMENTATION OF SUSTAINABILITY STRATEGY IN MEGAPROJECTS AND BEYOND IS THE DNA OF PROJECT TECHNOLOGY-BASED FACILITY MANAGEMENT.

TESTIMONIALS

I am so proud of our Emirati FM guru. I have known Ali for many years as we started to form the first FM non-profit association in the region, MEFMA. Ali's passion and commitment reflect consistently on the Middle East FM industry growth and maturity. You can depend on Ali for strategic FM and asset management expertise, especially when it comes to setting up sustainable operational strategy for megaprojects and beyond.

I recommend you grab a copy of his first book on FM and enjoy learning from his rich experience.

MARWAN BIN GHALITA
– RERA CEO, DUBAI LAND DEPARTMENT

I have known Engineer Ali for more than a decade as we started MEFMA, the first FM non-profit association in the region. Ali has shown show great commitment to the industry. His contribution to the recognition of the FM industry in the Middle East region is tremendous, driven by his passion. His book about FM in megaprojects is an encapsulation of his rich personal experience and will certainly guide the readers to form an FM strategy for any development, small or large.

MUSAD AL DAOOD
– CEO, RIYADH AIRPORT

It is with great anticipation I await Ali's pending book reflecting his 25-year journey to date in relation to the emergence of Facilities Management (FM) in the Middle East. In this regard, the opportunity to say a few words about Ali and my interaction with him over a great deal of that 25-year period gives me great pleasure. When Ali and I crossed paths many years ago, I was impressed not only by the knowledge of what then was a very new and innovative discipline that was little understood within UAE, but perhaps more importantly about the passion he shared with me for what we both believed was a strategic and business critical management discipline. That he recognized the potential that a True FM approach could offer the economic wellbeing of the UAE; the demand organizations that were investing in its future as an economic hub; and most importantly the people who would be required to ensure its sustainability was, at that time, visionary. It was however his passion, communication skills, grasp of the challenges ahead that drew me towards Ali as an individual to engage and support him. At that time, he was one of those individuals who acted as a catalyst to creating a professional infrastructure to support those individuals and organizations who had a desire to become part of the FM journey in UAE to build upon the work to professionalize FM that had at that time been achieved primarily in Europe and North America. From that early engagement between Ali and myself eventually emerged the Middle East Facilities Management Association (MEFMA) and the rest as they say is history. I therefore have no doubt that this book being authored by Ali will be one rich in knowledge gained not only from his diverse and varied experiences that he has enjoyed in the demand organizations that he has worked with across the UAE, but also the interactions and leadership that he has had across the region promoting a True FM philosophy and understanding. To those that take the opportunity to read its content, you will hopefully be equally enthused by the rich knowledge and experiences that he has shared within it. Enjoy the read and benefit accordingly.

STANLEY G MITCHELL
– FOUNDING CHAIRMAN, ISO 267 FACILITY MANAGEMENT

I started working with Ali in 2007 at Imdaad and continued the journey in the FM industry through the formation and amazing growth & success of our regional FM industry association MEFMA. His passion, leadership & determination has been key to the success of MEFMA and the FM industry in the region. His first book is a reflection of his commitment to share knowledge and contribute further to sustainable FM industry in the region and worldwide.

JAMAL ABDULLAH LOOTAH
– GROUP CEO, IMDAAD GROUP

When I originally met Ali in the summer of 2008, I was impressed by two important leadership skills. As a visionary, Ali constantly examines technology and solutions designed to advance the management of facilities around the globe. He focuses on how these technologies will improve the financial performance of buildings, as well as the corresponding benefit these solutions will bring to the environment and the larger community. The second valuable trait that Ali holds is his understanding that technology alone will not solve the future problems of building operations. He understands that the people operating (and the people occupying) those properties must embrace the new processes that come with technology. Ali very strongly understands that people must be part of the change process and he constantly focuses on how to keep stakeholders engaged and a part of this transition to truly "smart buildings". I am very excited to see your vision come to light in your book soon!

GEORGE BRILL
– FOUNDER AND CEO, TALISEN TECHNOLOGIES INC.

ACKNOWLEDGMENTS

Putting this book together was not an easy task because this is a reflection of my years of experience learning from the different roles I played in the different industries I served. I have always and continue to look at the future of cities and countries in our region and how to maintain and expand the various facilities sustainably.

I want to extend my gratitude for the support from and passion of my business and industry partner, Gagandeep Chhabra. Since we met back in 2007, he has always been there through my FM journey, as a brother, partner and person who believes in my leadership quality all the way. Thank you, Gagan.

I also want to acknowledge the trust and support I have received from George Brill, who supported me during the writing of this book. It was a blessing meeting him in 2008 and maintaining our friendship over the years. I truly consider him a brother and a mentor.

I am grateful for the guidance and support I received from the Passionpreneur tribe leader, Moustafa Hamwi. Thank you to the entire publishing team, especially Clare McIvor.

This book is a true reflection of my industry passion, ambition, and aspirations to drive future sustainable growth.

AUTHOR BIO

Ali Alsuwaidi is a passionate visionary FM leader. Throughout his career, he has been able to learn and share his knowledge, connect with leaders and experts, and proactively bring FM professionals and various stakeholders together. He energises individuals and organisations to improve and become agents of change. The most creative of leaders connect people and encourage them to see the big sustainable picture and achieve win-win situations for all involved stakeholders – Ali is an exemplification of this approach.

WORK WITH ME

I am available for FM strategy advisory services, coaching, conducting workshops and more. Please visit www.alialsuwaidi.com or write to ImpacfulFM@alialsuwaidi.com to get in touch with me.

Consulting assignments I am available for extend across strategic business growth and operational strategy areas:

- Foundational business thought
- Operational stabilisation and business growth services
- Ongoing operations advisory
- Construction, testing and commissioning stage works
- Technical audits and condition surveys
- Transition and handover management
- Preparation of bid documents for selection of service providers
- Bid management
- CAFM advisory
- Training

NOTES